The Sisters Gr
Spells and Charms for your Happily Ever After
By Bree NicGarran and Anna Zollinger

The Sisters Grimmoire is copyright © 2015 by Bree NicGarran and Anna Zollinger

This book is distributed in Paperback and Electronic format with DSRM enabled. All rights to this book and its content are reserved- this includes the right to reproduce this book or portions thereof in any format; no part of this book may be used or reproduced in any manner whatsoever- including internet usage- without written permissions granted by the author(s) except in the case of brief quotations embodied in critical articles or reviews, or in other manners, formats, and lengths congruent with Fair Use.

Neither Bree NicGarran nor Anna Zollinger endorse third party transactions outside of the designated sale channels, nor do they have any authority or responsibility concerning the unaffiliated third party resale of this material, or private party transactions between other members of the public. They shall not be held liable for the resale or redistribution outside of the designated sale channels. Those companies designated as the appropriate sale channels shall hold all responsibility for any problems with the book and its delivery.

Any references or sources contained within this work are current at the time of publication. The Author(s) cannot guarantee that these references or their locations and availability will continue to be maintained after publication. All external products or materials in this book are the property of and registered trademarks, products, etc. of the companies that produce them. The Author(s) makes no attempt to claim ownership or copyright over these products.

If you have purchased or received a copy of this book which reads PROOF on any area of it, you have obtained a limited supply early release copy; If you have received a redistributed copy of this book without a cover- or in an illegal electronic format that is not congruent with the formats distributed through parties designated for sale via the author(s): You should be aware that this book is likely stolen property and the Author(s) have not been fairly compensated for their work. Please consider donating the sale price of the book at the time of obtainment to the Author(s) through the appropriate channels in order to compensate for it.

If you have purchased or read this book, please consider reviewing its contents at Amazon.com or goodreads.com; direct all concerns or queries to the author(s)' Tumblr at http://breenicgarran.tumblr.com (Bree) http://agloriousbeauty.tumblr.com (Anna), or to their email at breenicgarran@outlook.com (Bree) and al.zollinger@yahoo.com (Anna)

Table of Contents

Acknowledgements
Preface: Into the Woods

Section One: Success and Prosperity
Foreword: Luck-Bringing and Money-Drawing

> **Straw Into Gold** *(Rumpelstiltskin)*; to bring wealth and opportunity
> **The Golden Tree** *(Cinderella)*; to bring financial gain when needed
> **The Buried Coins** *(The Golden Goose)*; to bring riches and good fortune
> **Shower of Gold** *(Frau Holle)*; to bring lasting wealth and prosperity
> **Table of Plenty** *(One-Eye, Two-Eyes, and Three-Eyes)*; to provide resources
> **Lentils In The Ashes** *(Cinderella)*; for help in solving a problem
> **On the White Duck's Back** *(Hansel and Gretel)*; for help passing an obstacle
> **The Wheel of Swords** *(The Iron Stove)*; to pass a difficult trial without harm
> **Ask the Woods** *(Iron Hans)*; to grant a wish with the help of land spirits
> **Wish Ball** *(The Crystal Ball)*; to grant your heart's desire

Section Two: Protection and Warding
Foreword: Wards and Shields

> **Don Thy Armor** *(The Owl)*; personal protection
> **Eyes Like Coals** *(The Bremen Town Musicians)*; creation of a house guardian
> **Lambkin's Blessing** *(The Lambkin and the Little Fish)*; protection of a child
> **Seven Little Acorns** *(The Wolf and the Seven Young Kids)*; deterring intruders
> **Spirit Net** *(Clever Else)*; warning of intruding spirits
> **The Bear** *(Snow-White and Rose-Red)*; protection against abuse and invective
> **Flower in the Hedge** *(Sweetheart Roland)*; protection against harm and bullies
> **The Glass Coffin** *(The Glass Coffin)*; the escape or rescue of another
> **Wall of Thorns** *(Little Briar-Rose)*; protection of home and property
> **What Big Teeth** *(Little Red-Cap)*; protection during travel

Section Three: Relationships and Romance
Foreword: On Attraction and Love Spells

    Spinning Up A Sweetheart *(Spindle, Shuttle, and Needle)*; to attract a partner
    The Apple and the Well *(The Frog King)*; to attract a companion
    The Ring and the Glass *(The Robber Bridegroom)*; to attract a spouse
    The Golden Apple of Life *(The White Snake)*; to kindle or renew romantic love
    Binding the Blades *(Sharing Joy and Sorrow)*; to create marital harmony
    Moon and Mill-Pond *(The Nixie in the Pond)*; to bring a loved one home
    Ever Faithful *(Faithful Johannes)*; to create or reinforce fidelity
    The Fiery Tongue *(Mary's Child)*; to gain a confession from an untruthful lover
    A Humble Pot *(King Thrushbeard)*; to humble an overly demanding lover
    The Bearded Doll *(King Thrushbeard)*; to curse another with love

Section Four: Glamour and Manipulation
Foreword: On Deception and Glamour Magic

    Mirror, Mirror *(Little Snow-White)*; glamour of physical beauty
    Odds and Ends *(The Hurds)*; a glamour of the ideal self
    Golden Bearskin *(The Gold-Children)*; to pass unnoticed
    Roughskin *(The Princess In Disguise)*; a protective disguise glamour
    The Fox's Gift *(The Sea-Hare)*; to hide magical workings
    Carrying the Fox *(The Fox and His Cousin)*; manipulate someone to help you
    Just Desserts *(The Raven)*; fool another into giving you control
    Hornet's Sting *(The Wren and the Bear)*; Trick someone to let you win
    Three Heads in a Knapsack *(The Trained Huntsman)*; to show that you're honest
    The Fowl in the Pot *(Clever Gretel)*; to get away with something
    Little Nettle Plant *(Maid Maleen)*; to break someone's glamour

Section Five: Revelation and Truth-Seeking
Foreword: Revelation and Truth Seeking

    Three Twigs In A Teacup *(The Shoes That Were Danced to Pieces)*; Tasseography
    The Poisoned Comb *(Little Snow-White)*; to reveal deception
    The Singing Bone *(The Singing Bone)*; reveal the misdeeds of another
    The Bird's Warning *(The Robber Bridegroom)*; warn another of danger
    The Three Ravens *(Faithful Johannes)*; household warning charm
    Three Golden Hairs *(The Devil with the Three Golden Hairs)*; solution to a problem
    Mirror of Truth *(The Crystal Ball)*; to discover another's true self
    Pennies in the Sun *(The Bright Sun Will Bring It to Light)*; bring the truth to light
    Little Grey String *(The Riddle)*; the answer to a question
    The Golden Ball *(The Frog King)*; locate a lost object

Section Six: Curses and Retribution
Foreword: On Baneful Magic

    Bite My Shiny Red Apple *(Little Snow-White)*; punish bothersome houseguests
    Into the Oven *(Hansel and Gretel)*; punish those who harm you
    Logs in the Fire *(The Old Witch)*; punish intrusive busybodies
    Bellyful of Stones *(The Wolf and the Seven Young Kids)*; punish a greedy person
    Mouthful of Flames *(The Pink)*; punish one who has slandered
    Out of the Sack *(The Table, The Ass, and the Stick)*; punish a thief
    The Bottle Trap *(The Spirit in the Glass Bottle)*; entrap and confuse
    Wicked Thorns *(Rapunzel)*; curse with blindness
    Drop the Millstone *(The Juniper Tree)*; revenge for a wrong
    Three Beatings A Day *(Cabbage-Donkey)*; revenge for magic used against you

Section Seven: Curatives and Spell Removal
Foreword: On Healing and Hexbreaking

    The Nesting Toad *(The Griffin)*; heal or to hex
    The Water of Life *(The Water of Life)*; assist with curing illness
    The Bloody Egg *(Fitcher's Bird)*; assist with healing an injury
    'Neath the Lime Tree's Shade *(The True Bride)*; heal heartache
    The Sorrow Pot *(The Goose-Girl)*; relieve sorrow and enact justice
    All Heads Off But Mine *(King of the Golden Mountain)*; reclaim power
    Seven-Year Bath *(Bearskin)*; remove magic from one's self
    The Red Flower *(Jorinde and Joringel)*; remove magic on another
    Twelve White Flowers *(The Twelve Brothers)*; remove magic on a group
    Drown the Witch *(The Foundling Bird)*; turn a curse back upon the caster
    Fearless in the Fire *(The Drummer)*; to break baneful magic

End: Last Notes and Suggested Reading
    Deriving Spells from the Analysis of Faery Tales
    Herbs for Cursing
    Herbs for Protection
    Herbs for Healing
    Herbs for Relationships
    Herbs for Opportunity
    Herbs for Divination and Truth Seeking
    Lunar and Solar Charts

Acknowledgements

I would like to extend my heartfelt thanks to all my followers on Tumblr, who have shown so much enthusiasm and support for the project, and are ever-ready to remind me that yes, this is in fact a great idea for a book. Gratitude and blessings also go out to all the wonderful people who promoted the project and contributed to our crowdsourcing fund. This would not have been possible without you.

I would also like to thank my sweetheart, my Ragnar, for his constant love and support (not to mention putting up with all those evenings I spent buried in my drafts), and longtime friend and sister-witch Jenna, for being the World's Greatest Sounding Board and for her invaluable input on several spells that had me temporarily stumped. And thanks to my parents as well for their moral (and financial!) support of the project despite our religious and ideological differences. It's always nice to rediscover the unconditional love of family.

Many thanks are also due to my fabulous co-author, Anna, for handling both the commissioning of the artwork and the practical aspects of publication, as well as contributing to the literary content and, perhaps the biggest challenge of all, keeping me on track. Truly a woman of many talents! Thanks are due also to Anna Beylenn for all her hard work on the beautiful cover art and interior illustrations.

And last but not least, I wish to thank my most stalwart supporter, my constant companion, and deliverer of on-demand fuzz therapy, Sir Havoc of Gingerdale, First of His Name, and Witchcat Extraordinaire.

See you all in Volume 2!

– Bree NicGarran

This book has truly taken me on a magical journey this year. So much so, in fact, that it is genuinely hard for me to begin at a single place without becoming completely overwhelmed by emotion. There are simply too many people that need to be thanked.

I want to thank my Husband; my shining beacon in the darkness who knows how to calm me down when my keyboard decides to go on the fritz again at 2am. His unconditional support and encouragement to discover what I love and take the first tentative steps to doing it has meant the world to me. I also have to thank my cats who have doled out much needed (if forcefully obtained) cuddles along the way. They may not be Witchcats like Bree's Havoc, but they have certainly been invaluable companions. My sanity may have truly been lost without these three in my life.

And Bree. Oh glorious, wonderful, extraordinary Bree who has dealt so amazingly with my feelings of inadequacy during this project; who has carried so much weight so graciously as my life has kicked into overdrive and spiraled places I never thought possible. I never thought that I would co-author a book, but I cannot possibly be happier with the opportunity to be doing it with such an absolutely extraordinary woman such as her- and I only hope that she has been as happy with me as I have been with her during this journey. It has been my privilege to be a part of her realizing her dream as an author. I hope to see many more books come from her hands- with or without my name next to hers. I know that she will write such amazing things!

And then there is the community; the support and generosity, the excitement. I could not have asked for more wonderful people to support me. I had been disillusioned for a very long time but your spirit has encouraged, nurtured, and revived my own. I owe so much to you that I will never be able to express my gratitude in simple words alone. I only hope and pray that the contents of this book and the plans to follow live up to your vibrant expectations.

May you always feel the sun upon your face (unless, of course, you're allergic).

- Anna Zollinger

Into the Woods

Contrary to certain beliefs, anyone can be a Witch- and Witchcraft is, of course, the art of such a person. It requires no initiation, no certain foundations, and no certain methodology unless you join one of the thousands of established Traditions and Practices which stipulate such things for their own groups and members (and to those who are not members of their groups, their stipulations do not apply despite any assertions that they do). Such an art is found in many cultures and many forms- from simple folk traditions to elaborate ceremonial ones; the spiritual and the non-spiritual; initiatory traditions, and ones which are not; those as old as time itself, and modern practices no older than 100 years or less. It is an ever evolving and ever growing art that more people pick up every day.

One of the most prevalent places Witchcraft- and Witches- are found, though, is in the common Faery Tales… Tales which often cross a multitude of cultural boundaries.

The history of Faery Tales is as long and complex as Human History itself. We have had these tales passed down to us from generation to generation for centuries- teaching us their morals, ethics, the working of life, and more. They can even teach us a little about Magic and Witchcraft if you only know where and how to look; to translate these stories into magical practice, spells, and charms, and weave them into fruition… But after stumbling across what paltry (and often problematic) Grimoires which exist concerning the use of Faerie Tales in modern Witchcraft, we were disappointed in the materials available to us. Thus, we were inspired to create our own.

The Sisters Grimmoire was started with a single thought: To breathe new life into some of our favorite stories and inspire others in return; to encourage the growth of a practice surrounding the Faery Tale and the wonderful potential it offers to those willing to look deeper at its meaning. Now we present you with a fun and inspiring collection of spells that every Witch will love.

This book- hopefully the first of many- features spells, charms, crafts, and more which are inspired by some of our most beloved stories from the Brothers Grimm; tales such as Sleeping Beauty, Hansel and Gretel, and Little Red Riding Hood, among others. We have dug our claws deep into the land of the Traditional Faerie Tale, poring over tales in order to pick themes, find symbolism, and retell these stories through the lens of Modern Witchcraft; to make something so many hold near and dear to their hearts, something so interwoven with our own histories, into something tangible…

Because these are more than just stories.

Luck Bringing and Money Drawing

Success magic is some of the easiest to cast, but it presents a unique challenge: the exception; an exception in a magical working is both a qualifier and a safeguard. These are usually employed in the unique situations where accidental harm might be done through the casting of magics which are otherwise meant to be beneficial to the caster or others.

In the specific instance of luck-bringing and money-drawing they can be especially tricky since the good fortune you ask for may come from an unexpected (and sometimes unwanted) source- such as an inheritance in the case of the death of a loved one. There might be also be a trade-off- such as getting a raise at your job, but the raise coming with more responsibility and more work.

Since everything we do affects others, and everything we ask for must come from somewhere, it is truly impossible not to do something that may harm someone in even a small manner. However, putting exceptions in place narrows the parameters of where your magically-summoned money or good luck will be pulled from. As a result, it helps to screen out the truly undesirable situations and avoid the most painful consequences or harm.

This is not to say that doing magic for personal gain is a bad thing, however! We are certainly not of the mindset that it will get you into trouble on some cosmic level, or that it is immoral, or any number of things. Using magic to help you acquire needed funds or achieve your goals is perfectly acceptable and there is ample evidence of people doing such castings throughout the course of Human history. Being a little clever in how you go about it never hurts, though. Indeed, it often comes with better results in our experience.

If you're concerned about the acquisition of luck or of funds causing harm to others, you can include a simple exception charm with your working. Simply chant or meditate upon the idea of the money coming from a harmless place, or stitch the intention into a charm bag included with your working. You may even use an incantation if you choose to, and such an incantation might be something along the lines of:

Needle, needle, weave your thread
And bind this spoken charm.
This spell will bring me what I need
And it will do no harm.

Straw Into Gold

The little man took the necklace, seated himself before the wheel, and whirr, whirr, whirr! three times round and the bobbin was full; then he took up another, and whirr, whirr, whirr! three times round, and that was full; and so he went on till the morning, when all the straw had been spun, and all the bobbins were full of gold.

Tale #055; **Rumpelstiltskin**

Intent: To bring monetary wealth to the caster.
Ideal Timing: Waxing or Full Moon

Materials:

Empty bobbins or spools x3	Small jar of any shape	Yellow or Green Candle
Yellow embroidery thread		Amber or Orange Oil

Most sewing or craft stores will sell empty spools or bobbins for sewing machines. Acquire three such spools or bobbins and enough yellow embroidery floss or sport weight yarn to fill them.

After sundown, light a candle (yellow or green is ideal, but white works also) and sit down with the bobbins and floss. Focus on the candle flame and think of the way in which you would like money to come into your life.

Once you have the idea firmly in mind, begin winding the floss slowly around the bobbin and continue until it is full. Repeat until you have filled all three bobbins, then blow out the candle.

Anoint the three bobbins with orange or amber oil, if you have it handy. Place them into a small jar and leave it somewhere it will not be disturbed. If the desired wealth does not come into your life within three months, or if you need more money, repeat the spell and add the three new bobbins to the jar.

The Golden Tree

As no one was now at home, Cinderella went to her mother's grave beneath the hazel bush, and cried, "Shiver and quiver, little tree, Silver and gold rain down on me." Then the bird threw down a dress of gold and silver, and a pair of slippers embroidered with silk and silver. And in all haste, she put on the dress and went to the festival. But her step-mother and sisters did not know her, and though she must be a foreign Princess, she looked so beautiful in her golden dress. Of Cinderella they never thought at all, and supposed that she was sitting at home, and picking the lentils out of the ashes.

Tale #021; **Cinderella**

Intent: To bring wealth to the caster as it is needed.
Ideal Timing: Full Moon

Materials:

Small cloth bag	Gold colored marker	Silver colored coins x2
Sewing needle	Gold colored thread	Gold colored coin
Orange Peel, Whole Almond, Sesame Seeds, Rice		

Acquire or make for yourself a small cloth bag in whatever color you like. With golden-colored thread, carefully sew the basic shape of a tree into the fabric. If you're not much of a hand at sewing, you may want to acquire a bag made of light-colored fabric and draw the tree on with a gold-colored marker instead.

On a full-moon night, fill the bag with a Dried Orange Peel, a Whole Almond, a Pinch of Sesame Seeds, a Palmful of Rice, two Silver-Colored Coins, and one Gold-Colored Coin if you can find it. Close the bag carefully. You may want to sew the top shut to keep the items inside.

If you ever need money, shake the bag three times over your head and say:

Shiver and quiver, little tree;
Silver and gold rain down on me.

The Buried Coins

And the Simpleton answered, "I have only a flour and water cake and sour beer; but if that is good enough for you, let us sit down together and eat." Then they sat down, and as the Simpleton took out his flour and water cake it became a rich pancake, and his sour beer became good wine. Then they ate and drank, and afterwards the little man said, "As you have such a kind heart, and shared what you have so willingly, I will bestow good luck upon you. Yonder stands an old tree; cut it down, and at its roots you will find something," and thereupon the little man took his departure. The Simpleton went there, and hewed away at the tree, and when it fell, he saw, sitting among the roots, a goose with feathers of pure gold.

Tale #064; **The Golden Goose**

Intent: To bring wealth and riches to the caster.
Ideal Timing: Waxing Moon

Materials:

Small cloth bag	Gold colored marker or pain	Pitcher of water
A feather	Handful of coins	Trowel

Make or acquire a small cloth bag. Place several coins of any denomination and one gold-colored feather (obtained by painting a feather gold, or my coloring it with a gold marker) inside the bag, and seek out a nearby tree. Larger, older trees will yield the best results but any tree will do. Carefully bury the bag beneath the roots of the tree. Do your best not to disturb the roots themselves and do NOT, under any circumstances, damage the tree.

Once you've buried the coins, lay both hands over the earth and say:

Here I lay my golden duck
The feather I'll return to pluck
The coins I'll give for further luck

For three days and three nights, bring water to the tree. Pour the water on the opposite side from where you buried the bag.

On the fourth day, return to the tree and dig up the bag. Remove the coins and give them to the first person you see on your way home. If you do not see anyone, donate the coins to charity. Keep the feather and place it in a jar or crock with your spare change to encourage growth and monetary gain.

Shower of Gold

Frau Holle took her by the hand and led her to a large door standing open, and as she was passing through it there fell upon her a heavy shower of gold, and the gold hung all about her, so that she was covered with it.

Tale #024; **Frau Holle**

Intent: To bring lasting wealth and prosperity to the caster for their kindness and hard work
Ideal Timing: Waxing Moon

Materials:

An Offering	Teapot or Pitcher	Cheesecloth
Chamomile, Marigold, Bergamot, Ginger, Marjoram		

Before performing this spell, it would be wise to make an offering of bread or apples. This can be in the form of leaving the food for local wildlife, or by donating the food to a local shelter.

For the industry portion, mix together 1 part Chamomile, 1 part Marigold, 1 part Bergamot, 1/2 part Ginger, and 1/2 part Marjoram. Create an infusion of the mixture by gently simmering 1 tsp of herbs per 1 cup water for approximately 15 minutes. Strain the resulting liquid through cheesecloth and into either a single serve Teapot or a Pitcher in order to remove the herbaceous material; paper towels will work as well if cheesecloth is unavailable, or- if you want to avoid the mess of straining altogether- you can sew the herbs into a coffee filter first.

Let the infusion cool to a skin-safe temperature. When it is cool to the touch, take a shower and very carefully pour the infusion over your head.

Table of Plenty

Then the wise woman said, "Wipe away thy tears, Two-eyes, and I will tell thee something to stop thee ever suffering from hunger again. Just say to thy goat "Bleat, my little goat, bleat. Cover the table with something to eat!" and then a clean well-spread little table will stand before thee, with the most delicious food upon it of which thou mayst eat as much as thou art inclined for. And when thou hast had enough, and hast no more need of the little table, just say "Bleat, bleat, my little goat, I pray, And take the table quite away. Then it will vanish again from thy sight." Hereupon the wise woman departed.

Tale #130; **One-Eye, Two-Eyes, and Three-Eyes**

Intent: To obtain only the needed money or provisions in dire times.
Ideal Timing: Waxing or Full Moon

Materials:

Piece of paper	A white candle	Tweezers
Writing utensil		Pinch of rice

Write what you need on the paper. The list can be as long or as short as you need it to be, but the more specific you are, the better the spell will work. Be sure that you only ask for what you really need. A little excess is fine, in case of something unexpected, but don't go overboard.

Fold the paper into a small packet with the rice inside and place it in a fire-safe dish. Light the white candle and carefully drip wax onto the packet, turning it until it is completely covered on all sides. I suggest using tweezers or a pencil to turn the packet so you don't burn your fingers.

As you drip the wax onto the packet, chant seven times:

Blessed rice and words of power,
Aid me in my needful hour.
Hear my cry, I pray you heed,
The help I ask comes not from greed.

Hide the packet away somewhere it won't be disturbed; if you have a few coins to hide with it in a jar or crock, so much the better.

Once your circumstances have improved and you are once more back on your feet, retrieve the packet and burn it in a fire-safe dish. Recite over the flames:

You gave me help when I had none;
You have my thanks, your work is done.

The spell may be repeated as often as you have need.

Lentils In The Ashes

At last, the step-mother said, "I have strewed a dishful of lentils in the ashes, and if you can pick them all up again in two hours you may go with us". Then the maiden went to the back-door that led into the garden and called out "O gentle doves, O turtle-doves, And all the birds that be, The lentils that in ashes lie, Come and pick up for me! The good must be put in a dish, The bad you may eat if you wish". Then there came to the kitchen-window two doves, and after them some turtle-doves, and at last a crowd of all the birds under heaven, chirping and fluttering, and they alighted among the ashes ... and began to pick, peck, pick, peck, and put all the good grains into the dish.

Tale #021; **Cinderella**

Intent: To help one complete a difficult project or task.
Ideal Timing: Waxing Moon, but can be performed anytime.

Materials:

A small but generous bag of Birdseed

When a task or a project seems impossible, cast this spell to give yourself a helping hand.

Buy a small bag of birdseed and go to a local park, or wherever wild birds gather in flocks. Throw out small handfuls of seed until a sizeable number of birds have gathered. Then hold in your mind the task that you need to complete and quietly say:

> *Little birds that fly so free,*
> *I pray you, lend your aid to me.*
> *The lentils in the ashes lie;*
> *Upon your help I must rely.*

Continue feeding the birds for several minutes, until they start to fly away. Scatter one more handful of seeds for any birds that might come later. When you leave, apply yourself to completing the task as best you can- and be on the lookout for any help that may come from unexpected sources while you do so.

On the White Duck's Back

When they had journeyed a few hours, they came to a great piece of water. "We can never get across this," said Hansel, "I see no stepping-stones and no bridge." "And there is no boat either" said Gretel; "but here comes a white duck; if I ask her she will help us over!" So she cried, "Duck, duck, here we stand, Hansel and Gretel, on the land, Stepping-stones and bridge we lack, Carry us over on your nice white back."

Tale #015; **Hansel and Gretel**

Intent: To help one pass a difficult obstacle.
Ideal Timing: Waxing or Full Moon for wish fulfillment, Waning or Dark Moon to remove obstacles.

Materials:

Piece of paper	A white feather	Gold Glitter
Writing utensil		Silver Glitter

This spell calls for a white feather, but it is not necessary that it be a duck's feather. You should be able to find a white feather at most craft stores. If you happen to find a white feather, however, we do not recommend that you pick it up and decide to use it. Feathers- especially plain ones- are hard to identify and items from a large number of bird species are illegal to possess under Federal Law no matter how they were obtained.

On the piece of paper, write down the goal that you're trying to obtain and the obstacles standing in your way. Be specific as you can. You can also include a list of things that would help to solve your problem or help you reach your goal. The more information you can provide, the better the spell will work.

Dip the feather in the glitter and gently shake it over the paper so that glitter falls upon the written words. Do this seven times, and as you do, say:

Dust of gold and feather white
Bring me to a future bright
I'm standing stranded on the shore
Carry me over to something more

Fold the paper up into a packet and tape the edges so that the glitter stays inside. Carry this in your pocket until the result you seek manifests in your life.

Wheel of Swords

Then he gave her three things, which she was to take the greatest care of, namely, three large needles, a plough-wheel, and three nuts. With these she traveled onwards, and when she came to the glass-mountain which was so slippery, she stuck the three needles first behind her feet and then before them, and so got over it, and when she was over it, she hid them in a place which she marked carefully. After this she came to the three piercing swords, and then she seated herself on her plough-wheel and rolled over them.

Tale #127; **Iron Stove**

Intent: To help pass a dangerous or painful experience with as little damage as possible.
Ideal Timing: This spell can be performed anytime.

Materials:

Sharp Knives x3	M/L Embroidery Hoop; no cloth	Darning Needle and Pins
Black Yarn	Paper and Writing utensil	Metal jump ring
8 each of Oak Twigs, Lavender Stalks, and Cinnamon Sticks		

Collect eight Oak twigs and eight Lavender stalks and trim them to a length equal to the radius of your hoop so that the herbs reach halfway across on the inside of it. Bind them together into eight bundles with the yarn and affix the cinnamon sticks to the center of the bundles, laying in direction with them. Set these aside.

To form your base for the wheel, start by using the black thread to wrap the entire circumference of your embroidery hoop so that none of the original hoop material shows. When you get to the end, tie off your string but do not cut it. Instead, starting where your string is mark of eight equidistant points around the circumference of the hoop with your pins in order to make your spokes.

Affix the jump ring to the black yarn so that the ring hangs positioned in the center of the wheel. Begin to wrap the jump ring with the yarn like you did with the hoop. However, instead of wrapping the entirety of the jump ring, stop after a couple wraps once you are in line with the pin for the next spoke. Pass the yarn up to the pin point and tie the yarn to the hoop with a half knot, being careful to ensure that the center jump ring stays positioned. Bring the yarn back down to the jump ring (wrap it a couple times around the first pass if necessary) and pass it through the ring. Repeat this step until all eight spokes are made. When you reach the end, tie off the string and cut it.

Next, grab one of the eight bundles of herbs. Thread your darning needle with the yarn and- starting at a spoke string- stitch into the wrapping of the large hoop (not the jump ring) on the underside of it so that your stitching is on the inside. Affix the her bundle to the spoke string by passing the yarn and needle through the binding on the Herb, around the base spoke string, and then back through the binding. Repeat until you have sewn the length of the bundle to the spoke string the secure the string to the jump ring at the end. Cut the yarn, then repeat this step for all other spokes until finished.

Your wheel is now complete! Write your full name- as well as any nicknames, magical names, or chosen names- on a piece of paper, fold it up, and tuck it into the center ring. If you feel it necessary, bind the name paper in place with yarn in order to hold it more securely.

Finally it is time to perform the spell.

Lay out the three sharp knives on a sturdy table or surface. Ensure that the blades are pointing away from you, and that you take any necessary safety precautions to prevent injury. Name each of them for one of your troubles, an obstacle you wish to overcome, or a coming experience that you're dreading.

Next, roll the wheel over the blades three times being careful not to snag or slice the yarn wrappings. As you do so, say:

O'er perils that before me lie,
This wheel my shield and comfort be
Until the troubles pass me by
And hold no power over me.

Hang the wheel in the window, place it on a shelf, or otherwise display it until such a time as the troubles named have passed. If you wish to do so, you may even decorate it with crystals, bells, seashells, feathers, or ribbons if you like at this time.

Ask the Woods

"As thou hast not a bad heart, and as I mean well by thee, there is one thing I will grant thee; if thou fallest into any difficulty, come to the forest and cry, 'Iron John,' and then I will come and help thee. My power is great, greater than thou thinkest, and I have gold and silver in abundance."

Tale #136; **Iron Hans**

Intent: To grant wishes with the help of land spirits.
Ideal Timing: Waxing Moon or Full Moon

Materials:

Slip of paper	White string	An Offering

This spell works best when a wish is being made for something that you need, rather than want. To increase the chances of this spell succeeding quickly, carry an offering with you into the woods. Some ideas for offerings are a pitcher of water for the trees, a handful of seed for the birds, apples for the deer; whatever you have handy so long as it is environmentally safe, as well as safe for wildlife to consume.

Write your wish on a slip of paper and fold it lengthwise. Cut several inches of white string and take both of these things with you into the woods with your offering. Seek out a Bay, Beech, Walnut, or Willow tree. Tie the folded paper to one of the branches with the string, saying:

*Stately tree, I stand below,
And what I seek, now you shall know.
I pray you, give me what I need,
For I am true in heart and deed.*

Leave your offering around the roots of the tree and go straight home without speaking to anyone. Go back to the tree one week later. If the paper is gone, your wish will be granted. If it is still there, you will be disappointed.

You can try the spell again if it hasn't worked, but you may want to rethink your wish or ask it of a different tree.

Wish Ball

When the youth went to the enchanter and held [the crystal ball] before him, the latter said, "My power is destroyed, and from this time forth thou art the King of the Castle of the Golden Sun. With this canst thou likewise give back to thy brothers their human form." Then the youth hastened to the King's daughter, and when he entered the room, she was standing there in the full splendor of her beauty, and joyfully they exchanged rings with each other.

Tale #194; **The Crystal Ball**

Intent: To create a charm to grant your wishes.
Ideal Timing: Full Moon

Materials:

Fillable craft ornament	Yarn or string to hang	Paper and writing utensil
See "Herbs for Opportunity" for Wishing based herb selection		

Firstly, obtain a fillable ball-shaped ornament. These can be obtained from craft stores during the winter holiday season, or online year-round.

Prepare a blend of herbs suited to your magical purpose. You may feel free to create your own specific blend for this one, and you will find a suggested list in the final appendices beneath "Herbs for Opportunity". Once you have your blend of herbs, fill the ornament about ½ to 3/4 of the way to the blend. Net write your wish on a small piece of paper and put it into the ball.

At this point you may feel free to decorate the ball however you wish; you can add decorations like sequins, glitter, jingle bells, or confetti to the inside, draw on the outside, or anything else you please. These charms are meant to be decorative, so be as artistic as you like.

When you are satisfied with your ornament, close the ornament and carefully shake it to combine the paper, herbs, and decorations. Hang the witch ball in a window or from a shelf, wherever it will be touched by sunlight at some point during the day.

Spell Creation Worksheet

Title of Tale: _____

Inspirational Passage: _____
_____
_____
_____
_____

Nature: _____ **Intent:** _____ **Target:** _____

Duration and Timing: _____

Materials: _____
_____
_____
_____

Casting Method: _____

Instructions: _____
_____
_____
_____
_____
_____
_____
_____
_____
_____

Notes: _____
_____

Spell Creation Worksheet

Title of Tale: _____

Inspirational Passage: _____
_____
_____
_____
_____

Nature: _____ **Intent:** _____ **Target:** _____

Duration and Timing: _____

Materials: _____
_____
_____
_____

Casting Method: _____

Instructions: _____
_____
_____
_____
_____
_____
_____
_____
_____

Notes: _____
_____

Spell Creation Worksheet

Title of Tale: _____

Inspirational Passage: _____

_____

_____

_____

Nature: _____ **Intent:** _____ **Target:** _____

Duration and Timing: _____

Materials: _____

_____

_____

Casting Method: _____

Instructions: _____

_____

_____

_____

_____

_____

_____

_____

_____

_____

_____

Notes: _____

_____

Spell Creation Worksheet

Title of Tale: _____

Inspirational Passage: _____
_____
_____
_____
_____

Nature: _____ **Intent:** _____ **Target:** _____

Duration and Timing: _____

Materials: _____
_____
_____

Casting Method: _____

Instructions: _____
_____
_____
_____
_____
_____
_____
_____
_____

Notes: _____
_____

Wards and other Protections

Warding and Shielding techniques are some of the most basic magical methods and spells which are employed by many a Witch- though some methods can certainly be difficult to learn at first. Ultimately their goal or purpose is that of protection; to stave off either physical or magical harm, ill will, or misfortune which may befall whatever is being protected against such things- whether it is a person, place, item, animal, or another thing that these spells are cast on.

These methods come in a very wide range of styles- from bottles and jars, to visualization techniques, charms and crafts, and more. We have done our best to illustrate this variety, as well as offer a swath of protections for different circumstances during which they may be useful for a practitioner. Wards and Shields may have additional non-protective purposes, as well, but we've chosen to focus predominantly on their protective uses in keeping in line with the themes throughout various Faery Tales.

It is important to recognize, however, that protections have limitations- and that these limitations come in both metaphysical and physical forms.

In terms of these physical limitations, the protective spell is often simply another barrier to discourage or lessen the chance or ability- but it does not always prevent it. Having that additional mundane barrier in place certainly helps and we believe that a magical protection should not take the place of physical precautions except in the event that there are no mundane options which are available or practical.

Two examples which come to mind are Storm Wards and Door Wards- both for the protection of a house from damage or loss in different way. A ward against storm damage does not wholly prevent any and all damage from occurring and it should also not mean that you no longer take the preventative measures available in order to decrease the opportunity for damage to occur (such as moving the trashcans to a safe location, and other measures). Likewise, warding your door in no way means that there is no longer a reason to continue locking it. You should still continue to lock your door despite having a ward in place.

When it comes to metaphysical limitations, though, these limitations are usually on how many hits that a protective spell can protect against before fizzling out finally. If you find that your protection charms or jars have burst or broken- particularly after you notice a lot of narrow escapes, it may be that the charm has reached the end of its effectiveness.

An example is that of a woman who contacted Bree about a protection charm for her husband - a snowplow driver. He had narrowly avoided more than a dozen accidents and slips in a single snowy night, then came home only to discover that his wife's protective charm bag had burst. The bag bursting is well within the realm of possibility, especially if it had a very hardworking night as it sounds like it did. This sounds to us like a protection spell meant to stave off accidents and trouble doing exactly what it is supposed to do, and then finally reaching the end of its rope when it had a months' worth of trouble in one single shift.

Ultimately it does pay to make protection charms as strong as possible, but that doesn't mean that they don't have limits and shelf lives. When bags or jars for protection spells break, it generally means that they've reached their limit and will need to be remade, especially if they're going to be doing high-capacity work.

Don Thy Armor

He ordered them to give him some armor, had a sword and spear brought, and armed himself. All praised his courage, though many feared for his life.

Tale #174; **The Owl**

Intent: To protect oneself from harm with magical armor.
Ideal Timing: This spell can be performed anytime.

There are many methods of putting magical protections in place. The most basic and most portable method is the personal shield, also called a personal ward. This is a protective magical barrier which moves and travels along with you and can generally be raised or lowered at will- or simply set "on" at all times- in order to protect yourself from magical or metaphysical harm.

If you wish to link an additional set of personal shields to a particular item of clothing or jewelry, that can be done as well. Some witches even link personal wards to tattoos or permanent piercings. Ultimately, however, this is a very easy and very effective way of keeping yourself safe requires no tools, incantations, or physical talismans to be effective.

While standing in a power stance (good, confident posture; straight backed, shoulders back, head forward, legs shoulder width apart, etc), begin by taking a moment to center yourself if you feel it necessary. Once you have, remain in the power stance and take a few deep breaths to clear your mind as much as you can.

Picture your energy as best as you can, but make sure that when you do that you picture it as something malleable and flexible; some people use water for this visualization, others fire, some light or shadow, and so on. Once you have that image set in your mind, cup your hands together in front of your stomach and picture that energy pouring into your hands and pooling there.

Breathe deeply and bring your hands out as if you were to take a weapon and shield from another person, focusing on the flow of the energy as you do so. Picture that energy expanding and forming into the weapon and shield that you seek to take. Once the visualization is set, bring your hands back to your chest with another deep breath. Now picture that energy expanding further to cover your body entirely and settling to form a coat of armor over yourself.

Imagine the details of your weapon, shield, and armor. Make it as small or large, as detailed or as simple as you wish. Imagine that this moves with you, bends with you, expands and contracts as needed, though; it is armor but it should never be confining to you. Now pour your will into it and imagine that nothing gets past this armor unless you want it to.

Be aware that energy work like this takes a great amount of energy and concentration. It doesn't always work out the way you want it to the first few tried; sometimes it is best to start small, especially if this is your first shield. We recommend regularly practicing creating, raising, and lowering your shields- perhaps as part of a meditation exercise. The hope, though, is to eventually make it as vivid as you can; to be able to focus on that image until you can picture it vividly and clearly in your head at a moment's notice and can almost feel it on the palms of your hands when you hold them out. Once you have the method down for getting the shield into place, you can raise it anytime and anywhere you need to at a moment's notice.

Eyes Like Coals

When midnight drew near, and the robbers from afar saw that no light was burning, and that everything appeared quiet, their captain said to them that he thought they had run away without reason, telling every one of them to go and reconnoitre. So one of them went, and found everything quite quiet. He went into the kitchen to strike a light, and taking the glowing fiery eyes of the cat for burning coals, he held a match to them in order to kindle it. But the cat, not seeing the joke, flew into his face, spitting and scratching.

Tale #027; **The Bremen Town Musicians**

Intent: To create a guardian spirit which will defend the home from intruders.
Ideal Timing: Full Moon

Materials:

Glass bottle or jar	Rusted or bent pins x10	Cat fur or claw
Juniper Berries, Red Peppercorn, Cumin, Hot Pepper of Choice		

This spell creates a guardian spirit to look after your home. You will need to feed and keep it to a certain extent as you would with any other creature sharing your living space. It will also be important to notify the guardian spirit of anyone who is allowed to be in the home when you're not there, such as friends or family or housesitters, otherwise the spirit may take any interloper as a potential threat and try to drive them out.

In a glass bottle or small jar combine a pinch of cumin, a spoonful of red peppercorn, a palmful of juniper berries, and the seeds of any red pepper of choice. Add the pins, and cat fur or claw; if a real cat is not available for donations of fur or claw, a simple picture of a cat can be placed into the container. Something ferocious-looking would be appropriate.

Take the jar around the house and touch it to all the exterior doorjambs and windowsills. As you do, speak softly to it:

Eyes like coals of burning fire
Let all intruders taste your ire
Claws as hard and sharp as steel
Here and gone, but feeling real
If uninvited in they come
With tooth and claw, defend our home

Leave the jar where it won't be disturbed, or bury it beside your doorstep. A planter pot may be employed for the burial, if desired.

If you move away at a later date you will need to either take the jar with you. If you do not plan on taking it with you, simply retrieve the jar and empty it while saying the following incantation in order to dismiss the spirit.

Sheathe your claws, the battle's won.
The home is safe, your job is done.
Be on your way, O Wild Heart,
Now go in peace; in peace, depart.

Once finished, simply cleanse and store the jar away. Feel free to reuse the jar at a later date for another House Guardian if needed.

The Lambkin's Blessing

When the cook heard that the lambkin could speak and said such sad words to the fish below, he was terrified and thought this could be no common lamb, but must be bewitched by the wicked woman in the house. Then said he, "Be easy, I will not kill thee," and took another sheep and made it ready for the guests, and conveyed the lambkin to a good peasant woman, to whom he related all that he had seen and heard. The peasant was, however, the very woman who had been foster-mother to the little sister, and she suspected at once who the lamb was, and went with it to a wise woman. Then the wise women pronounced a blessing over the lambkin and the little fish, by means of which they regained their human's forms, and after she took them both into a little hut in a great forest, where they lived alone, but were contented and happy.

Tale #141; **The Lambkin and the Little Fish**

Intent: To protect a child from danger or bewitchment.
Ideal Timing: Full Moon

Materials:

Woolen baby yarn	Material focus (if possible)	Cloth poppet or doll
Sewing needle	Muslin bag (optional)	Sewing thread
Lamb's Ear or Mullein Leaf, plus Dairy, Caraway Seed, and Flax Seed		

This spell creates a type of poppet known as scapegoats. These are poppets which are created to absorb and nullify baneful magic in order to protect the person it represents. In this case, you'll create one for a child.

Make or acquire a cloth poppet and cut a hole into its torso (or simply leave a hole, if sewing it yourself). Combine three leaves of Lamb's Ear (or substitute Mullein) with a dried Daisy blossom and several pinches each of Caraway and Flax seeds. If you happen to have a strand of the child's hair or a nail clipping or a baby tooth, add that as well. If these things are not available, you can use a photograph; a simple name slip is not a strong enough association for this type of spell. Once you are finished, stuff the herb blend into the torso of the poppet, and sew up the hole.

Take the woolen yarn and tie nine knots into it. As you do, invest each knot with the power to ward off some kind of harm or misfortune. These can be as vague or specific as you need them to be and you can customize the knot blessings to whatever you think is best for that particular child. An example is as follows:

May no harmful magic touch you.
May your friends be loyal and understanding and true.
May your illnesses be short and easily cured.
May your booboos be nothing that a band-aid can't heal.
May you never be hungry without food to fill your belly.
May no violence touch you, within the home or without.
May no hand be laid upon you to cause you grief.

Once all the knots are made, tie the yarn around the poppet and charge it by saying:

Poppet, I charge you to defend the life and heart of [Child's Name].
You stand as their guardian, your flesh is their shield.
What harm would come to them, you shall turn away.
Poppet, I command you, stand ready!

Saying the child's name before each line, repeat the nine blessings over the poppet once more.

Alternatively, if you cannot create or obtain a poppet, instead obtain a doll (the more it looks like the child, the better) and a muslin bag. Fill the bag with the herbs and material focus as instructed in the standard poppet method, then close the bag.

After performing the steps to create the knotted yarn, use the yarn to affix the poppet to the doll's torso. Perform the rest of the spell as instructed.

Regardless of whether you use the standard method or the alternative, after all this is done, tuck the poppet away somewhere it won't be disturbed so it can watch over the little charge and do its' work. You may even tuck it under their mattress for a few nights while they sleep in order to amplify the scapegoat's connection to the child.

Seven Little Acorns

But who should come in but the wolf! They were terrified and wanted to hide themselves. One sprang under the table, the second into the bed, the third into the stove, the fourth into the kitchen, the fifth into the cupboard, the sixth under the washing-bowl, and the seventh into the clock-case.

Tale #005; The Wolf and the Seven Little Kids

Intent: To protect against home invasion.
Ideal Timing: This charm can be performed anytime.

Materials:

Black thread or yarn	Acorns x7	Whole bay leaves x7

Take together seven acorns (if you cannot get acorns, then simply acorn caps will do) and seven large bay leaves. Wrap the Acorns in the bay leaf, and then wrap them again with a thick black thread or yarn. If the bay leaves are too stiff for wrapping, they can be soaked in water until soft, or you can carefully sew the acorn to the hard leaf.

Hide each of the seven acorns in a different location around the house to protect from home intrusion and unwanted company. Make sure to place at least one acorn in each room if possible. If there are more than seven rooms, then concentrate on placing them in whichever rooms are the most important focal points of your house.

This spell should be refreshed once or twice a year to keep your home intruder-free.

Spirit Net

But when evening came and she still stayed away, Hans went out to see what she had cut, but nothing was cut, and she was lying among the corn asleep. Then Hans hastened home and brought a fowler's net with little bells and hung it round about her, and she still went on sleeping. Then he ran home, shut the house-door, and sat down in his chair and worked. At length, when it was quite dark, clever Elsie awoke and when she got up there was a jingling all round about her, and the bells rang at each step which she took. Then she was alarmed, and became uncertain whether she really was clever Elsie or not, and said, "Is it I, or is it not I?" But she knew not what answer to make to this, and stood for a time in doubt, at length she thought, "I will go home and ask if it be I, or if it be not I, they will be sure to know." She ran to the door of her own house, but it was shut, then she knocked at the window and cried, Hans, is Elsie within. "Yes," answered Hans, "she is within."

Tale #034; **Clever Elsie**

Intent: To warn of the presence of spirits in one's home.
Ideal Timing: This charm can be created at any time.

Materials:

A large amount of Yarn	Small bells	A 40" long rod or stick
Sea Salt, Clover, Garlic, Basil, and Catnip		

Take a skein of heavy weight yarn in any color (though yellow, gold, or earth tones may be best) and cut 10 pieces at least 80 inches- or approximately 6 ½ feet- in length. Soak these in a solution of Sea Salt, Clover leaf, Garlic, Basil, and Catnip overnight, then allow them to air dry.

When the yarn is dry, double each piece over on itself so that it becomes a "single" string 40 inches in length. Create a single-loop knot at the end of the length of yarn where you doubled it over on itself (not the two open ends), so that you have a loop followed by a knot and two loose ends. When doing this, make sure that the loop made by the single-loop knot you created is large enough to fit around your chosen rod. Repeat this step with the other nine lengths of yarn so that you have 10 rod sized loops and 20 loose ends.

Place the loops onto your rod and space them evenly apart from one another. Adjust the knots as necessary so that they are secure.

This next step is easier if you have somewhere (like a wall mounted rack for coats) on which to hang the rod, but it can be done just as easily sitting on the floor. Using a square knot, begin to create a net using the instructional image on the following page; if you need clearer instructions they can easily be found online.

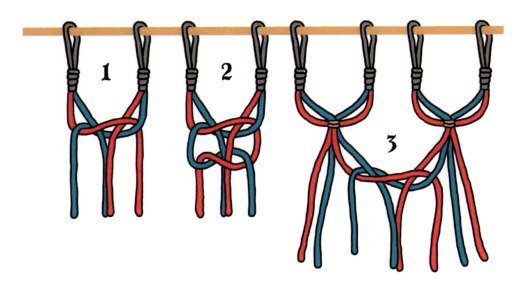

After step three, simply use step 2 to finish the knot. Repeat this, working your way down the rows until you have a completed net. When it is finished, affix the bells to each knot on the web.

Hang this anywhere in the house you wish- though it is advisable to avoid hanging the net in the way of breezes from doors, windows, or air ducts, or in places where people or pets might bump against it. When properly hung, the net will warn you when spirits are near.

The Bear

[The dwarf] was going on with his bad words when a loud growling was heard, and a black bear came trotting towards them out of the forest. The dwarf sprang up in a fright, but he could not get to his cave, for the bear was already close. Then in the dread of his heart, he cried, "Dear Mr. Bear, spare me, I will give you all my treasures; look, the beautiful jewels lying there! Grant me my life; what do you want with such a slender little fellow as I? You would not feel me between your teeth. Come, take these two wicked girls, they are tender morsels for you, fat as young quails; for mercy's sake eat them!" The bear took no heed of his words, but gave the wicked creature a single blow with his paw and the dwarf did not move again.

Tale #161; **Snow-White and Rose-Red**

Intent: To protect oneself from harm and abuse.
Ideal Timing: Waxing Moon to Full Moon

Materials:

Small cloth bag		Bear charm
Basil, Fennel, Hyssop, Peppermint, and Vervain		

This spell requires a bear figurine small enough to fit in your pocket. The material, color, and decoration are up to you, but you'll want something durable. Stone, wood, plastic, crystal, resin, whatever you can find as long as it's not likely to break or fall apart.

Create a charm bag with generous pinches of Basil, Fennel, Hyssop, Peppermint, and Vervain. Place the bear figurine inside the bag and hold it tightly in your hands. Put your mouth close to the bag and whisper to the bear; tell it your situation, tell it what you're afraid of and who is hurting you. Finish by saying:

Bear, my shield, my sword, my arm,
Who holds your image, none may harm.

Take the bear from the charm bag and carry it in your pocket. Leave the bag of herbs under your mattress or in whatever place feels safe for you as added protection.

The Flower in the Hedge

Then the maiden and her dear Roland took again their natural shapes, and traveled on the whole night through until daybreak. Then the maiden changed herself into a beautiful flower, standing in the middle of a hedge of thorns, and her dear Roland into a fiddle-player. It was not long before the witch came striding up, and she said to the musician, "Dear musician, will you be so kind as to reach that pretty flower for me?" "Oh yes," said he, "I will strike up a tune to it." Then as she crept quickly up to the hedge to break off the flower, for she knew well who it was, he began to play, and whether she liked it or not, she was obliged to dance, for there was magic in the tune. The faster he played, the higher she had to jump, and the thorns tore her clothes, and scratched and wounded her, and he did not cease playing until she was spent, and lay dead.

Tale #056; **Sweetheart Roland**

Intent: To protect yourself or someone you love from someone who means to do you harm.
Ideal Timing: Waning Moon

Materials:

Jar with a tight lid	Poppet	Pins, needles, and tacks
Palmful of Salt		

Tale your poppet and- if you are able to obtain a material focus for the poppet- stuff it into the chest cavity. If a focus is not available, you can use a name slip or name the poppet thus:

Poppet, I name you [Name]. Your limbs are their limbs, your flesh is their flesh. As you suffer, so shall they suffer, according to my will.

If the target is an unknown person, the poppet can be named Danger or Threat.

In the jar, combine half of the pins with the salt. Put the poppet inside on top of the pins, then pour the rest of the pins on top to form a loose cage. Whisper into the jar:

On your feet, it's time to dance;
With the music, jump and prance.

Cap the jar and seal the lid tightly.

Select a song with a good dancing beat and shake the jar to the beat for as long as you can. If you can make it through the whole song, do so; if not, shake for as long as you can. The idea is that as the poppet "dances," it is pierced by the pins in the jar.

Set the jar aside somewhere that it won't be disturbed. Whenever the target gives you trouble, take the jar out, turn on the music, and shake the poppet full of pins. If at any point you feel the target has learned their lesson, retrieve the poppet from the jar, take out any pins stuck into it, and remove the focus or dunk the poppet in salt overnight to neutralize the spell.

The Glass Coffin

The tailor was looking at the beauty with beating heart, when she suddenly opened her eyes, and started up at the sight of him in joyful terror. "Just Heaven!" cried she, "my deliverance is at hand! Quick, quick, help me out of my prison; if you push back the bolt of this glass coffin, then I shall be free." The tailor obeyed without delay, and she immediately raised up the glass lid, came out and hastened into the corner of the hall, where she covered herself with a large cloak. Then she seated herself upon a stone and [...] it began to rise up on high with the maiden and the young man, and mounted through the opening of the ceiling into the upper hall, from whence they then could easily reach open air.

Tale #163; The Glass Coffin

Intent: To bring opportunities for escape or rescue to someone trapped in a bad situation.
Ideal Timing: Full Moon, but this spell can be cast anytime.

Materials:

Red Apple	Bucket or bowl of water	Empty Bucket or bowl
Whole Cloves			

Find a watertight bucket or basin. It doesn't have to be very large, just large enough to float an apple. Prepare another bucket or pitcher full of water. Take a red apple and hold it in your hands. Name the apple and charm it thus:

> *[Name], you are trapped in a coffin of glass,*
> *But with this fruit of bloody red,*
> *You'll quickly out of danger pass*
> *And safely shall you rest your head.*

Gently place the apple in the empty bucket, then pour water into the bucket so that the apple floats up to the top. Leave the bucket and the floating apple in the sunlight for an hour, then rescue the apple and give it to the person for whom it is named.

The spell works best when the person in need of rescue consumes the charmed apple. If there is some reason they cannot or will not eat the apple, plant it in the earth or a planter pot instead.

If you wish the charm to work in secret, stick the rescued apple full of whole cloves and leave it somewhere dry to work its' magic over time.

The Wall of Thorns

Then round that place there grew a hedge of thorns thicker every year, until at last the whole castle was hidden from view, and nothing of it could be seen but the vane on the roof. [...] From time to time many Kings' sons came and tried to force their way through the hedge; but it was impossible for them to do so, for the thorns held fast together like strong hands, and the young men were caught by them, and not being able to get free, there died a lamentable death.

Tale #050; **Little Briar-Rose**

Intent: To protect one's home and property.
Ideal Timing: Full Moon, but can be made anytime.

Materials:

Glass jar with a lid	Black candle	Super glue and ducktape
Planter pot	Planting Soil	Pins and / or thorns
Your Urine or Vinegar or Lemon or Pickle Juice, Dill, Basil, Salt		

Fill the bottle with the pins, herbs, and just enough of the urine to fill the bottle about 3/4 of the way; if you are uncomfortable using your own urine (as is traditional for Witches' Bottles) then add the Pickle or Lemon Juice- or even vinegar, which is just as effective.

Seal the top and secure with a strip of duct tape or electrical tape to prevent leaks. Once it is sealed well, begin to attach the flat ends of the thorns to the outside of the bottle using the superglue so that the points face outward. Be very careful not to stick yourself while handling the bottle!

Once all the thorns are in place, light the black candle and drip the wax over the top of the bottle. As the wax falls, hold the image of a thorny protective barrier in your mind and continue to turn the bottle- letting the wax spill down the sides to help hold the thorns in place. Keep dripping the wax until the cap is completely covered and all the thorns have been secured.

Pour some dirt into the planter pot, place the bottle inside, and pour in more dirt until the bottle is covered. Keep the pot somewhere on your property. You can even grow flowers in it, if you like, but I wouldn't recommend using it for anything edible.

If you move, be sure to take the pot with you, or dig up the bottle and take it along; to remove the ward, break the wax seal and empty the contents of the bottle somewhere safe.

What Big Teeth

Now the grandmother lived away in the wood, half an hour's walk from the village; and when Little Red Riding Hood had reached the wood, she met the wolf; but as she did not know what a bad sort of animal he was, she did not feel frightened.

Tale #026; **Little Red Cap**

Intent: To protect oneself during travel.
Ideal Timing: This charm can be made anytime.

Materials:

A tooth	Red thread or ribbon	Rose water or oil
	A red cloth bag	
Ash wood, Cinquefoil		

Obtain for yourself a tooth which you can fit in your pocket. The tooth may be of any sort, but sharp and pointy is preferable. If you do not wish to use an actual animal tooth, you can make one out of white modeling clay or salt dough.

With a red string or ribbon, bind the tooth together with a sprig of Ash and a sprig of Cinquefoil. Place all this in a small red cloth bag and anoint with three drops of rosewater or rose oil. Holding the bag in your hands, picture yourself as fierce as the creature whose tooth lies within and say aloud:

Here I stand in my red hood
You think me sweet, you think me good.
But beware of what can lie beneath
I may seem soft, but I have big teeth.

This will create an aura of intimidation around the carrier which will- in turn- discourage malice or harm. In order for it to work, simply carry it with you when you travel.

Spell Creation Worksheet

Title of Tale: _____

Inspirational Passage: _____
_____
_____
_____
_____

Nature: _____ **Intent:** _____ **Target:** _____

Duration and Timing: _____

Materials: _____
_____
_____

Casting Method: _____

Instructions: _____
_____
_____
_____
_____
_____
_____
_____
_____

Notes: _____
_____

Spell Creation Worksheet

Title of Tale: _____

Inspirational Passage: _____

_____

_____

_____

Nature: _____ **Intent:** _____ **Target:** _____

Duration and Timing: _____

Materials: _____

_____

_____

Casting Method: _____

Instructions: _____

_____

_____

_____

_____

_____

_____

_____

_____

_____

Notes: _____

_____

Spell Creation Worksheet

Title of Tale: _____

Inspirational Passage: _____

_____

_____

_____

Nature: _____ **Intent:** _____ **Target:** _____

Duration and Timing: _____

Materials: _____

_____

_____

Casting Method: _____

Instructions: _____

_____

_____

_____

_____

_____

_____

_____

_____

Notes: _____

_____

Spell Creation Worksheet

Title of Tale: _____

Inspirational Passage: _____
_____
_____
_____

Nature: _____ **Intent:** _____ **Target:** _____

Duration and Timing: _____

Materials: _____
_____
_____

Casting Method: _____

Instructions: _____
_____
_____
_____
_____
_____
_____
_____
_____
_____

Notes: _____
_____

Love and Attraction

Love Spells are the second most controversial form of magic within the community. Indeed, it's with good reason: What if the person you call might be what you think your ideal partner is, but that turns out to be wrong? What if they turn out to be the exact opposite of what you want, and only put on that pleasant face in the public eye?

These are valid questions which may seem extreme to ask, but on the internet the Witchcraft and related communities are filled with stories wherein a person performs a Love Spell only to have it work in a manner that is less desirable- though technically within the realm of how it could have worked without the spell being considered a "failure". These results have been everything to stalking, harassment, overly jealous lovers, to abuse, obsession, and many more which are both unpleasant and often endangering.

Another aspect of love magic which makes it highly controversial is the nature of some of the spells to begin with. An overwhelming number of these available spells - and the spells often requested of us - are targeted spells which by their very nature are questionable and interfere with a person's free will in various manners, some of which have lead certain portions of the community to compare the practice to assault, and with good reason

Ultimately Love Magics (in our experience) have the largest potential to backfire on the caster with much more dire results when they do- more so than even cursing. It is fickle, tricky, complicated, and can turn 50 Shades of "Oh No" in an instant. In the words of The Aunts, "Be careful what you wish for."

This does not mean that we do not advocate the usage of Love Magics. We take the stance that while there are many ways to do Love Magic incorrectly, there are also plenty of ways to do a Love Spell right- and therefore with little risk of negative backlash or the use of targeted spells that are questionable in nature. We especially find that it is much easier and less questionable to use "seeking" spells in order send out a call for the qualities you want in a partner without having a specific person in mind. This allows for a lot more wiggle room and can lead to some pleasantly surprising results as both Anna and Bree have experienced personally. The important thing, though, is that you mustn't expect instant results and should follow up your spellcasting with action; you cannot just sit around and wait for the right person to fall into your lap, you have to go out and look!

However, we've included more than just Love Spells within this section. You will also find spells to diffuse marital problems, as well as several others aimed at the existing family or spouse; there is a wide variety of spells within this section which cover several different aspects of one's relationships, both romantic and otherwise.

Spinning Up A Sweetheart

"Spindle, my spindle, haste, haste thee away, And here to my house bring the wooer, I pray. Shuttle, my shuttle, weave well this day, And guide the wooer to me, I pray. Needle, my needle, sharp-pointed and fine, Prepare for a wooer this house of mine." Hardly had the needle put in the last stitch than the maiden saw through the window the white feathers of the Prince, whom the spindle had brought thither by the golden thread.

#188; **Spindle, Shuttle, and Needle**

Intent: To bring someone into your life- to be roommate, lover, or spouse- who is the perfect person (or as close to perfect as possible) that you are searching for.
Ideal Timing: During the Waxing Moon leading up to the Full Moon.

Materials:

White or red thread	Empty Spool or Bobbin	Darning Needle
Red wine or juice	Embroidery hoop	Needle case

Day One: Soak the thread in red wine or juice, then wind it onto the bobbin once and tie it in a knot so that it holds tight. Swing the bobbin nine times around your head and envision the kind of person you're seeking. Hold the qualities and traits you're looking for in your mind as you wind the rest of the thread onto the bobbin.

When it is dry, hold the free end of the thread and roll the bobbin down a hallway or a flight of stairs. Let it unravel as much as possible. The further the bobbin goes, the farther the spell will travel to find that ideal person. Leave the thread undisturbed overnight. If you find in the morning that the thread has been moved, untie it from the bobbin and start over the following day with a new piece of thread.

Day Two: Wind up the thread again and use it to weave a web in an embroidery hoop. Use as much of the thread as you can- using a darning needle to help you if need be. Again, hold the qualities and traits of that ideal person in your mind as you work.

Day Three: Using the needle case to prevent sticking yourself with the needle, put the darning needle in your pocket and tidy up the house in anticipation of your partner's arrival. After that, there's nothing to do but wait for the person to come into your life. You will know them by the appearance of three white things of the same kind which coincides with their arrival.

The Apple and the Well

As she was thus lamenting, someone called out to her, "What is the matter with you, princess? Your crying would turn a stone to pity." She looked around to see where the voice was coming from and saw a frog, who had stuck his thick, ugly head out of the water. "Oh, it's you, old water-splasher," she said. "I am crying because my golden ball has fallen into the well." "Be still and stop crying," answered the frog. I can help you, but what will you give me if I bring back your plaything?" "Whatever you want, dear frog," she said, "my clothes, my pearls and precious stones, and even the golden crown that I am wearing". The frog answered, "I do not want your clothes, your pearls and precious stones, nor your golden crown, but if you will love me and accept me as a companion and playmate, and let me sit next to you at your table and eat from your golden plate and drink from your cup and sleep in your bed, if you will promise this to me, then I'll dive down and bring your golden ball back to you."

Tale #001; **The Frog King**

Intent: To find a companion or friend with whom to share your life (not necessarily romantic).
Ideal Timing: Waxing Moon

Materials:

Cup of water	An apple of any color	Gold paint
A bowl of any shape	Tealight candle	Paint brush

Fill a cup with water and set to the side of the bowl. In small increments, core the top of the apple- regularly checking to make sure that the tealight fits without being too loose or too low. When the top of the tealight sits flush with the top of the apple, stop.

On four sides of the apple paint the silhouette of a frog in gold. If you have no great artistic skill, writing the word "FROG" on each side of the apple in golden paint shall suffice. Allow the paint to dry on the apple while you paint a circle in the center of the bottom inside of the bowl. Allow it to dry as well.

Once all the paint is dry, place the tealight inside the hole you cored in the top of the apple. Place the apple in the bowl so that it stands erect with the tealight at the top. Light the tealight and fill the bowl with the water from the cup you gathered earlier.

Place the bowl somewhere safe away from any curtains or other flammable materials, then turn off all the lights. Sit before the bowl and meditate on the candle flame while thinking of the qualities you want in a platonic companion. When finished, blow out the candle.

Repeat every night until the time that the apple begins to spoil, refreshing the candle when necessary, until you are satisfied.

The Ring and the Glass

No sooner was it settled than the wicked gang entered the house. They brought another young woman with them, dragging her along, and they were drunk, and would not listen to her cries and groans. They gave her wine to drink, three glasses full, one of white wine, one of red, and one of yellow, and then they cut her in pieces. The poor bride all the while shaking and trembling when she saw what a fate the robbers had intended for her. One of them noticed on the little finger of their victim a golden ring, and as he could not draw it off easily, he took an axe and chopped it off, but the finger jumped away, and fell behind the cask on the bride's lap. The robber took up a light to look for it, but he could not find it.

Tale #040; **The Robber Bridegroom**

Intent: To draw a lover, with the intent of marriage.
Ideal Timing: Full Moon

Materials:

Red wine	Gold ring that fits	White candle

Light a white candle and poor yourself a glass of red wine to your taste. Drop a yellow or gold ring into the glass (ring does not have to be real gold) and drink the wine while thinking of the qualities you want in a spouse. Do not finish it, but leave a bit of wine in the glass at the end.

Holding the glass so that it is reflected in the light of the candle, look into the remaining wine at the ring and say:

> *Where is the finger that belongs to this ring?*
> *I wish to draw them hither!*

Repeat this as many times as you are comfortable before removing the ring from the remaining wine and placing it on your own finger. Remove the ring once you have entered into a relationship.

The Golden Apple of Life

When he had gone through three kingdoms he came one evening to a wood, and seated himself under a tree to go to sleep; but he heard a rustling in the boughs, and a golden apple fell into his hand. Immediately three ravens flew towards him, perched on his knee, and said, "We are the three young ravens that you delivered from starving; when we grew big, and heard that you were seeking the golden apple, we flew over the sea to the end of the earth, where the tree of life stands, and we fetched the apple." Full of joy the young man set off on his way home, and brought the golden apple to the King's beautiful daughter, who was without any further excuse. So they divided the apple of life, and ate it together; and their hearts were filled with love, and they lived in undisturbed happiness to a great age.

Tale #017; **The White Snake**

Intent: To rekindle love between two agreeable parties and contribute to a lasting relationship.
Ideal Timing: Full moon, but can be performed anytime.

Materials:

Yellow apple	A small jar with a lid	Sharp knife
Clover, Raspberry Leaf, Valerian Root			

This spell is meant to be cast with the help of your beloved.

Acquire a yellow or gold-colored apple. Any variety will do, as long as it's something you'll both be willing to eat. Throw the apple into the air three times and make sure you catch it. Once the spell begins, the apple must not touch the ground.

After the third catch, cut the apple in two and give half to your beloved. Together, pronounce the following incantation:

> *Who shares this golden apple with me*
> *Shall ever true and loving be;*
> *And I in turn do vow to be*
> *Ever good and true to thee.*

Eat the apple halves and save the seeds from the center. Place apple pips in a jar with name slips and spoonfuls each of Clover, Valerian, and Raspberry leaf.

Binding the Blades

There was once a tailor, who was a quarrelsome fellow, and his wife, who was good, industrious, and pious, never could please him. Whatever she did, he was not satisfied, but grumbled and scolded, and knocked her about and beat her. As the authorities at last heard of it, they had him summoned and put in prison in order to make him better. He was kept for a while on bread and water, and then set free again. He was forced, however, to promise not to beat his wife any more, but to live with her in peace, and share joy and sorrow with her, as married people ought to do.

Tale #17 **Sharing Joy and Sorrow**

Intent: To encourage marital communication and harmony.
Ideal Timing: Full Moon, for harmony and wish fulfillment.

Materials:

Large pair of scissors	Lavender oil	Measuring Tape
1 yard each of Red, White, and Gold yarn		

Take a pair of scissors or shears and anoint them with Lavender oil. With a measuring tape or yard stick, measure out 1 yard (3 feet) apiece of Red, White, and Golden yarn. Wrap the shears with the yarn while saying the following incantation:

I try to please and yet you hark and tease consistently
From now until my complaints are heard and joy returns
You shall share my sorrow.

Place the shears beneath the matrimonial bed and do not remove them until your marital problems have been corrected. When they are fixed, simply remove the scissors and unwrap them, then dispose of the yarn.

The Moon and the Mill-Pond

"Be comforted," said the old woman, "I will help thee. Here is a golden comb for thee. Tarry till the full moon has risen, then go to the mill-pond, seat thyself on the shore, and comb thy long black hair with this comb. When thou hast done, lay it down on the bank, and thou wilt see what will happen."

Tale #181; The Nixie in the Pond

Intent: To bring a lover safely home from far away.
Ideal Timing: Full Moon

Materials:

Shallow bowl of water	A comb	Spool of white thread
Small embroidery hoop	Oil and food coloring	Dropper bottle

To bring a lover safely home, sit before a bowl of water on the night of the full moon. Try to arrange the bowl so that the light of the moon falls upon it, if possible.

Take the white thread and weave a web in the embroidery hoop, filling in as much of the space as you can. Whistle or hum or sing a tune as you do so, particularly if you and your sweetheart happen to have a special song.

Once you've finished the web, set it aside the bowl. Drip a few drops of the food coloring onto the surface of the water and swirl them with the comb to make a loose spiral pattern. When you are satisfied, dip the hoop carefully into the water, and bring it up so that the colored oil catches on the white threads. Set the hoop aside and allow it to dry.

Hang the hoop in a window where the sun can shine upon it. Leave it there until the color fades from the thread or your lover returns home, whichever happens first.

Ever Faithful

There was once upon a time an old king who was ill and thought to himself 'I am lying on what must be my deathbed.' Then said he 'tell faithful John to come to me.' Faithful John was his favorite servant, and was so called, because he had for his whole life long been so true to him.

Tale #006; **Faithful Johannes**

Intent: To create fidelity in love, either for yourself or for a straying partner.
Ideal Timing: Full Moon

Materials:

Paper	Gold paint	Salt, Ashes, and dirt
Red thread or yarn		A key of any type

Gather a piece of drawing paper and gold paint. On it paint a picture of an Iris flower. If you don't have much artistic ability, you can cut or print out a picture of an Iris flower, glue it to the paper, and trace over it with the gold paint.

When you are done, sprinkle some ash, sea salt, and dirt over the painting. While doing so, recite the following as many times as necessary before painting the same phrase below the iris.

Faithful [name]

Allow the picture to dry then fold it as small as you can. Secure it with a red thread and key charm (or an old key you no longer have use for), and place it under your mattress.

The charm is particularly effective if your partner sleeps in the same bed.

The Fiery Tongue

A trial was held, and as she was not able to respond and defend herself, she was condemned to be burned at the stake. Wood was piled together. After she had been bound tightly to a stake, and the fire was beginning to burn around her, the hard ice of pride melted. Her heart was moved by regret, and she thought, "If only I could confess before my death that I opened the door." Then her voice came back to her, and she cried out loudly, "Yes, Mary, I did it!" Immediately rain began to fall from heaven, and it put out the fiery flames. A light broke forth above her, and the Virgin Mary descended.

Tale #003; **Mary's Child**

Intent: To garner a confession from a deceitful lover
Ideal Timing: Full Moon or Dark of the Moon

Materials:

A whole strawberry	A Knife	Matches
A sturdy fire safe dish		

Take a book of matches and a Strawberry. Halve the strawberry, and lay it fresh flat half down in a firesafe container. Poke a match straight up into the rounded outer side of one half so that it is protruding from the strawberry and light the match.

While the match is burning, recite the incantation:

> *I know the truth but you disagree;*
> *These lies shall be your pyre.*
> *Yet the truth can set you free,*
> *And release you from the fire.*
> *So confess your sin, confess to me,*
> *Or else you'll burn a liar.*

Allow the match to burn down until it extinguishes itself, then dispose of the match and strawberry either in the garbage, or outside in a safe area.

The Humble Pot

Her struggles did not help. He pulled her into the hall. But the string that tied up her pockets broke, and the pots fell to the floor. The soup ran out, and the scraps flew everywhere. When the people saw this, everyone laughed and ridiculed her. She was so ashamed that she would rather have been a thousand fathoms beneath the ground. She jumped out the door and wanted to run away, but a man overtook her on the stairs and brought her back. And when she looked at him, it was King Thrushbeard again. He said to her kindly, "Don't be afraid. I and the minstrel who has been living with you in that miserable hut are one and the same. For the love of you I disguised myself. And I was also the hussar who broke your pottery to pieces. All this was done to humble your proud spirit and to punish you for the arrogance with which you ridiculed me." Then she cried bitterly and said, "I was terribly wrong, and am not worthy to be your wife". But he said, "Be comforted. The evil days are past. Now we will celebrate our wedding."

Tale #052; **King Thrushbeard**

Intent: To humble a demanding lover, or to stop a verbally abusive one.
Ideal Timing: Dark of the Moon

Materials:

A small clay pot	Gold paint	Piece of charcoal
Black yarn		Red candle

If you cannot obtain a clay pot, you may create a pot using a simple salt dough recipe- however, make sure that you create one large enough for the piece of charcoal to fit in. When it is finished, allow to dry (or bake dry if your instructions say to do so). Once the pot is complete, light the red candle and paint the pot gold in color. Wrap the charcoal in the thread and place it in the pot.

Hold your hands over the pot and recite:

> *Your words bite like venom in my veins,*
> *And ring like screams within my ears.*
> *Now may your own tears fall like rain,*
> *And your own screams shall you hear.*
> *All so that you may know my pain,*
> *And humble yourself before me.*

Using the wax from the candle, tip it over the opening of the pot and allow the wax to drip into it. Seal it as best you can (or just cover the charcoal and thread), and allow the wax to cool.

Set this out in the sunlight for 24 hours to charge. When it is finished, take the pot, then, out to a sidewalk or other concrete structure, and throw it so as to break it. Carefully- and safely- collect all of the items and shards, the dispose of them in the garbage.

The Bearded Doll

Once the king sponsored a great feast and invited from far and near all the men wanting to get married. They were all placed in a row according to their rank and standing. First came the kings, then the grand dukes, then the princes, the earls, the barons, and the aristocracy. Then the king's daughter was led through the ranks [...] And thus she had some objection to each one, but she ridiculed especially one good king who stood at the very top of the row, and whose chin had grown a little crooked. "Look!" she cried out, laughing, "He has a chin like a thrush's beak." And from that time he was called Thrushbeard. Now the old king, seeing that his daughter did nothing but ridicule the people, making fun of all the suitors who were gathered there, became very angry, and he swore that she should have for her husband the very first beggar to come to his door.

Tale #052; **King Thrushbeard**

Intent: To make a scornful person get what they deserve in love.
Ideal Timing: Dark of the Moon

Materials:

White cloth	Stuffing material	Sewing needle
Hair from the target	Yarn of the target's hair color	Black thread

From the cloth create a poppet of the person you wish this spell to affect and sew it together with the black thread. Leave a small opening to place the stuffing into the doll and- if you are using their hair- place their hair inside before sewing it up.

If you are not using their hair, cut some yarn of the same color to appropriate lengths, and sew it on using the black thread so that it resembles the person's own hair style. Additionally, you may use scrap fabric to create raggedy clothing for the doll to wear if you choose.

Once you are finished, hold the poppet in your hand and recite:

Your song is sweet,
But your deeds bite like venom.
May you have the first you greet,
For all that you deserve.

Hide the poppet in a location where it will not be disturbed. If you decide to have pity at some later date, take the doll out and burn it to release the person from the spell.

Spell Creation Worksheet

Title of Tale: _____

Inspirational Passage: _____
_____
_____
_____

Nature: _____ **Intent:** _____ **Target:** _____

Duration and Timing: _____

Materials: _____
_____
_____

Casting Method: _____

Instructions: _____
_____
_____
_____
_____
_____
_____
_____
_____

Notes: _____
_____

Spell Creation Worksheet

Title of Tale: _____

Inspirational Passage: _____
_____
_____
_____
_____

Nature: _____ **Intent:** _____ **Target:** _____

Duration and Timing: _____

Materials: _____
_____
_____

Casting Method: _____

Instructions: _____
_____
_____
_____
_____
_____
_____
_____
_____
_____

Notes: _____
_____

Spell Creation Worksheet

Title of Tale: _____

Inspirational Passage: _____
_____
_____
_____
_____

Nature: _____ **Intent:** _____ **Target:** _____

Duration and Timing: _____

Materials: _____
_____
_____

Casting Method: _____

Instructions: _____
_____
_____
_____
_____
_____
_____
_____
_____
_____

Notes: _____
_____

Spell Creation Worksheet

Title of Tale: _____

Inspirational Passage: _____

_____

_____

_____

Nature: _____ **Intent:** _____ **Target:** _____

Duration and Timing: _____

Materials: _____

_____

_____

Casting Method: _____

Instructions: _____

_____

_____

_____

_____

_____

_____

_____

_____

_____

Notes: _____

_____

Glamour and Manipulation

Manipulations are any magic which seeks to trick another person into doing, believing, seeing, or otherwise perceiving something that you wish them to. Glamours are a type of manipulative magic, but they specifically affect ones' perception- usually their sense of sight.

Like Cursing and love Magics, manipulation magic is a hot button topic within the community. There is heated debate concerning the willful manipulation of others- though Glamour is often regarded as far more acceptable despite being a form of such magic. Even then, though, there are several people who believe that even Glamours should not be used for anything other than to either render yourself "invisible" to people, or to enhance others' perceptions of any natural, pre-existing traits or capabilities that you have.

Faery Tales, however, often contain instances of Glamour and Manipulation- not all of which have happy endings wherein the manipulated figure it out before it's too late. For all of their appearances within tales, we've chosen to include several different types with various purposes within this book, including some which may be controversial due to messing with free will- a no-no to several practitioners of varying traditions.

It is important to remember, however, that these tales also show us that there are limitations to such magic. The main limitation is it being noticed. In many cases, once someone figures out the Glamour or manipulation it breaks the spell entirely and the magic is rendered useless. When this happens sometimes it can have dire consequences for the caster. We see this especially often in tales involving those who can see the Fae Folk- though we've chosen not to include such spells in the Grimmoire.

Even without someone seeing through the Glamour there can still be certain problems that arise. With invisibility Glamours, for instance, tales abound about people who cast such spells upon themselves or their cars, only to end up injured in an accident because someone didn't see them there. It is important that fail safes for instances like this be put in place during the casting in order to prevent injury to you or the item that is Glamoured.

Mirror, Mirror

"Mirror, Mirror, on the wall, Who's the fairest of us all?"

Tale #053; **Little Snow-White**

Intent: To increase beauty and self-confidence.
Ideal Timing: Full Moon

Materials:

A tray or a cardboard box lid	Cloth bag	Evening primrose oil
Orange and / or Myrtle Blossoms, Rose Petals of any color, and Magnolia Blossoms		

In the springtime, go to the country and gather the blossoms of the magnolia tree. These huge white and pink-tinged blossoms are generally easy to find, even in some suburban areas. If you live in an area where orange or myrtle trees are common, these blossoms may be collected also. Lay the blossoms out to dry until they are completely stiff and crunchy; a shallow cardboard box or tray works very well for this.

Put the petals into a cloth bag. Add to this bag some rose petals in your choice of color and three drops of Evening Primrose oil.

Hang the bag over the first mirror you see each morning. Generally, this is going to be something in your bedroom or bathroom. Every day when you wake up, take a moment to touch the bag, look into the mirror, and smile at yourself.

While you're going through your morning routine before the mirror (brushing your teeth, shaving, applying makeup, etc.), choose one thing to love about yourself that day, no matter how small it is. Add new things to love every day until you realize that you are, in fact, gorgeous from head to toe, inside and out.

Remember: You are already beautiful. If other people can't see it, that's their problem.

Odds and Ends

There was once upon a time a maiden who was pretty, but idle and negligent. When she had to spin, she was so out of temper that if there was a little knot in the flax, she at once pulled out a whole heap of it, and strewed it about on the ground beside her. Now she had a servant who was industrious, and gathered together the bits of flax which were thrown away, cleaned them, span them fine, and had a beautiful gown made of them for herself. A young man had wooed the lazy girl, and the wedding was to take place.

Tae #156; **The Hurds**

Intent: To create a glamour of charm and beauty or for self-improvement.
Ideal Timing: Waxing Moon or Full Moon

Materials:

Jar with a tight lid	Paper and writing utensil	Magazines
Scissors	A large bowl	Jewelry piece of any kind
Rose Oil or Rose Water, plus a handful of dried Rose Buds		

This spell works with a very standard type of wearable glamour which attaches the spell to a small accessory or item of jewelry. This particular version works with beauty and charm, but it can easily be adapted for other effects; it can also be attached to cosmetics as well. Just make sure the item you wish to use can fit inside the jar- or, if necessary, get a bigger jar to fit the item.

The base for the glamour is a jar filled with personal traits you wish to enhance or acquire in the eyes of others. The jar component for this spell can be prepared two ways: words or pictures, whichever works best for you, and the methods may be combined as you see fit.

For visual work acquire a stack of disposable magazines. Clip out images of the things you wish to include in your glamour. If you wish to use words only, you can still clip titles or passages from periodicals, or you can type or write the words and phrases relevant to your glamour.

Once you have a collection of traits for your glamour, place all the clippings in a large bowl. Add a handful of dried rosebuds or rose petals. Red, yellow, or white are the ideal colors, but the roses can be any color you happen to have available. Stir the roses and clippings together until well combined, being careful not to disintegrate the dried flowers. As you stir, envision yourself as you wish to be seen or known.

Pack the clippings and roses into a jar which is large enough to hold the whole mix plus the anchor object. If you wish, you can add a few drops of rose oil or rosewater to enhance the manifestation of the spell. Hold the jar in your hands and say, in your head or aloud, the traits this charm will impart. Use affirmative phrases instead of speculative ones. (Say "I am" instead of "I will be.")

Leave the jar to sit overnight, then remove the anchor object. Wear the anchor whenever you have need of your created glamour. If you feel the spell is starting to wane or wear thin, simply place the anchor back in the jar overnight to recharge.

Golden Bearskin

But the other rode forward and reached a great forest. As he was about to enter it, the people said "it is not safe for you to ride through, the wood is full of robbers who would treat you badly. You will fare ill, and when they see that you are all of gold, and your horse likewise, they will assuredly kill you". But he would not allow himself to be frightened, and said, "I must and will ride through it." Then he took bear-skins and covered himself and his horse with them, so that the gold was no more to be seen, and rode fearlessly into the forest. When he had ridden onward a little he heard a rustling in the bushes, and heard voices speaking together. From one side came cries of, "There is one," but from the other, "Let him go, 'tis an idle fellow, as poor and bare as a church-mouse, what should we gain from him?"

Tale #085; **The Gold-Children**

Intent: To disguise oneself as unassuming; a spell for perceived invisibility.
Ideal Timing: Waning or Dark Moon

Materials:

Gold Embroidery Thread	Sauce pan	Coffee Filter x1
Embroidery Needle	Garment of choice	A bowl
Poppy Seeds, Cloves, and Basil		

Simmer 1 tbsp of the herb mixture per 1 cup of water on low heat for about 15 minutes, then remove from the heat and let it cool. Strain the infusion through a coffee filter to remove the herb material. Additionally, if you wish to cut out the straining process, simply place the herbs inside the coffee filter and sew it shut, then simmer it in the water.

Place the bowl outside overnight in the light of the moon to set. The next day, remove the string from the water and allow it to dry.

Once dried a fair amount, take a garment of your choice (though items such as scarves, handkerchiefs, and socks are preferable) and, in a corner or area of the garment where it will be unseen, embroider the silhouette of a small bear. Darker-colored clothing is best for this step.

Wear the garment whenever you feel you will need to go unnoticed.

Roughskin

"Before I consent to your wish, I shall require three things - a dress as golden as the sun, another as silvery as the moon, and a third as glittering as the stars; and besides this, I shall require a mantle made of a thousand skins of rough fur sewn together, and every animal in the kingdom must give a piece of his skin toward it" [...] In the night, when every one slept, she rose and took from her jewel-case a gold ring, a gold spinning-wheel, and a golden hook. The three dresses of the sun, moon, and stars she folded in so small a parcel that they were placed in a walnut shell; then she put on the fur mantle, stained her face and hands black with walnut-juice, and committing herself to the care of Heaven, she left her home.

Tale # unknown; **The Princess in Disguise**

Intent: To protect and disguise oneself from those who mean to harm you.
Ideal Timing: Full Moon, for protection, but can be performed anytime.

Materials:

Small patchwork cloth bag	Personal material anchor	Glue and a rubber band
Empty Walnut Shell halved, Dogbane, Hyssop, Basil, Heather, Juniper Berries, and Poppy Seed		

Obtain an empty walnut shell. You can use the shells off of the whole bagged walnuts that most grocery stores carry in the produce section. Try to crack the walnut so that the shell comes away in two halves. This makes reassembling it for the charm much easier.

In small pinches, mix the Dogbane, Hyssop Heather, Basil, Juniper Berries, and Poppy Seed together, then carefully stuff the herb mixture into the two empty halves of the walnut. Use little dots of glue to help the herbs stay in place. At the very last, add a strand of your hair or a nail clipping.

Line the edges of the shell with glue and carefully fit them back together. Wrap them with the rubber band to keep everything in place until the glue dries. Once the charm is dry, place it in a patchwork cloth bag. You can purchase one or make it yourself. It only has to be large enough to hold the walnut.

Hold the bag between your palms and say:

I garb myself in many skins
To keep harm out and safety in
I place the truth within this shell
Now guard my life and guard it well

You can either carry the bag with you whenever you feel you need protection, or you can hide the bag in a wooden box if one is available.

The Fox's Gift

On the last day, he went with a heavy heart into the country, and met the fox. "Thou knowest how to find all kinds of hiding-places," said he; "I let thee live, now advise me where I shall hide myself so that the King's daughter shall not discover me." "That's a hard task," answered the fox, looking very thoughtful. And length, he cried, "I have it!" and went with him to a spring, dipped himself in it, and came out as a stall-keeper in the market, and dealer in animals. The youth had to dip himself in the water also, and was changed into a small sea-hare. The merchant went into town, and showed the pretty little animal, and many persons gathered together to see it. At length, the King's daughter came likewise, and as she liked it very much, she bought it, and gave the merchant a good deal of money for it. Before he gave it over to her, he said to it, "When the King's daughter goes to the window, creep quickly under the braids of her hair". And now the time arrived when she was to search for him. She went to one window after another in turn, from the first to the eleventh, and did not see him. When she did not see him from the twelfth either, she was full of anxiety and anger, and shut it down with such violence that the glass in every window shivered into a thousand pieces, and the whole castle shook.

Tale #191; The Sea-Hare

Intent: To hide your workings so that they cannot be detected until their work is done.
Ideal Timing: Dark of the Moon, for concealment and deception

Materials:

Clam shell	Paper	Writing utensil
Black candle		Jar with a tight lid
Blueberry Leaves, Cherry Pits, and Poppy Seeds		

Write the name of the spell you wish to conceal on a slip of paper. If the spell does not have a name, simply write the type or intention of the spell and the date you cast it. Place the paper in a small glass jar with a handful of Blueberry Leaves, Cherry Pits, and Poppy Seeds. Hold the jar to your mouth and whisper:

> *Now you see it, now you don't*
> *Long you'll seek, but find you won't*
> *Ever hidden from your view*
> *Seen by me, but not by you*

Spit into the jar for extra potency, then screw the lid onto the jar. Light the black candle and drip wax onto the lid until it is mostly covered. Press the shell into the liquid wax concave-side-down to keep the spell hidden.

This will not hinder the effects of the spell you already cast, just keep it from being detected until it has accomplished what it needs to do. This is ideal for manipulation and baneful magics, as well as any spell that you wish to keep hidden for reasons of stealth. Once the spell has done its' work, remove the shell, open the jar, and discard the contents. The jar can be cleansed with salt or water and used for future magical workings. Be sure to remove the wax from the lid before cleansing.

Carrying the Fox

A dog was lying there, and it made such a noise that the peasants came running out, caught Gossip Wolf, and poured a strong burning mixture, which had been prepared for washing, over her skin. At last she escaped, and dragged herself outside. There lay the fox, who pretended to be full of complaints, and said, "Ah, dear Mistress Gossip, how ill I have fared, the peasants have fallen on me, and have broken every limb I have; if you do not want me to lie where I am and perish, you must carry me away." The she-wolf herself was only able to go away slowly, but she was in such concern about the fox that she took him on her back, and slowly carried him perfectly safe and sound to her house.

Tale #074; **The Fox and His Cousin**

Intent: To manipulate someone into helping you no matter the cost to themselves
Ideal Timing: Waxing Moon

Materials:

Paper	Writing utensil	Chicken feather
Material focus	Sugar	Black ribbon

Take a sheet of paper and on it in the center draw a fox standing on all fours. If you have no artistic ability simply writing the word "FOX" will suffice.

Place a chicken feather and something of the person you are manipulating (hair, skin, nails, or image being preferable) centered into the paper. Once done, sprinkle on a bit of sugar and fold it together.

Wrap the packet with a black ribbon and say:

Ill that I have fared and perish I shall,
But with your help I should be spared through efforts of a greatest pall.

Place the paper packet somewhere it won't be found or disturbed until such time as your situation has improved and you no longer need the target's help. Remove the focus and flush it down the toilet, then burn or flush the paper. The ribbon may be retained and cleansed with salt for future workings.

Just Desserts

One of [the thieves] said that he had found a stick, and that when he struck a door with it, that door would spring open. The next said that he had found a mantle, and that whenever he put it on, he was invisible, but the third said he had found a horse on which a man could ride everywhere, even up the glass-mountain. And now they did not know whether they ought to have these things in common, or whether they ought to divide them. Then the man said, "I will give you something in exchange for these three things. Money indeed have I not, but I have other things of more value; but first I must try yours to see if you have told the truth". They put him on the horse, threw the mantle round him, and gave him the stick in his hand, and when he had all these things they were no longer able to see him. So he gave them some vigorous blows and cried, "Now, vagabonds, you have got what you deserve, are you satisfied?"

Tale #093; **The Raven**

Intent: To fool someone into giving you power or control over a situation.
Ideal Timing: Dark of the Moon

Materials:

Small jar and a container	Mortar and Pestle	Paper and writing utensil
A large Marshmallow, Sugar, Powdered Cinnamon and / or Galangal Root		

Write your target's name on a slip of paper, or a brief description of the situation over which you want control. Use the end of a pen to punch a hole in a marshmallow. Roll the paper into a cylinder and stuff it into the hole you just made.

Fill a small jar partway with sugar. Place the marshmallow inside and top off the jar with more sugar. Store the jar somewhere dry and relatively cool which is out of direct sunlight.

Check on the marshmallow daily for signs of drying. When it is completely dried out and brittle, remove it from the jar and grind it into a powder with the mortar and pestle. Add a few pinches of the sugar from the jar and a generous pinch of either Ground Cinnamon or Galangal Root powder. Blend the ingredients thoroughly and bottle the mixture.

Sprinkle the mixture where you know your target will walk for full effectiveness. If this is not possible, you can bind up a spoonful of the powder with the name slip inside a paper charm packet and seal it with black wax and your thumbprint.

If the powder is deployed by the night of the full moon, you should see the target's power decrease with the waning of the moon while yours increases to replace it.

The Hornet's Sting

When day broke, and the battle was to begin, all the four-footed animals came running up with such a noise that the earth trembled. The willow-wren also came flying through the air with his army with such a humming and whirring, and swarming, that everyone was uneasy and afraid; and on both sides they advanced against each other. But the willow-wren sent down the hornet, with orders to get beneath the fox's tail, and sting it with all his might. When the fox felt the first sting, he started so that he drew up one leg, with the pain, but he bore it, and still kept his tail high in the air; at the second sting, he was forced to put it down for a moment; at the third, he could hold out no longer, and screamed out and put his tail between his legs. When the animals saw that, they thought all was lost, and began to fly, each into his hole, and the birds had won the battle.

Tale #102; The Wren and the Bear

Intent: To trick someone into giving up a fight or an argument, even if they're winning.
Ideal Timing: This spell can be cast anytime.

Materials:

A pin	A potato	A knife
Yellow modeling clay	A candle	Black modeling clay

Acquire some modeling clay in black and yellow, and a small pin; a pushpin or a thumbtack will do. Build a hornet-shaped figurine around the pin, leaving the sharp end exposed as the stinger. Let the clay dry until the figurine is solid.

Next, find yourself a potato and carve it with the name of the person you're trying to fool. Light the candle and carefully pass the carved side of the potato over the flame three times.

Take the hornet and "sting" the potato three times. As you do so, picture the target losing their words and their will to continue the fight, turning tail and running if need be. Whatever means that you will win the fight and they will lose.

Continue this daily until you get your way or the potato begins to turn mushy, whichever comes first.

Three Heads in a Knapsack

He had put on the sword with which he had cut off the heads of the three giants, and thus entered the hut, and ordered something to eat to be given to him. He was charmed with the beautiful maiden, who was indeed as lovely as any picture. She asked him whence came and whither he was going, and he said, "I am roaming about the world." Then she asked him where had got the sword, for that truly her father's name was on it. He asked her if she were the King's daughter. "Yes," answered she. "With this sword," said he, "did I cut off the heads of three giants." And he took their tongues out of his knapsack in proof.

Tale #111; **The Trained Huntsman**

Intent: To prove one's word is true
Ideal Timing: Full Moon

Materials:

Red paper	Regular paper	writing utensil
Scissors	Tape	

It is important to note, in the context of this faery tale, that the spell will only work if you have actually done what you say you have. A lie or even a stretching of the truth will show immediately and will have consequences. Only use this spell if you have been entirely honest.

On a sheet of paper, write a brief description of the situation. Be specific as to what really happened or is happening. Cut three small strips of red paper, just big enough to write on. On the strips, write the following:

I Speak The Truth
You Hear The Truth
All Shall Know The Truth

Place the red strips on the larger sheet of paper and fold the whole thing into a packet small enough to fit into your pocket. Tape it shut if need be. Stick to your guns and carry the packet with you the situation is resolved.

The Fowl in the Pot

When the one chicken was gone, and her master still had not yet returned, she looked at the other chicken and said, "Where the one is, the other should follow. The two belong together. What is right for the one, can't be wrong for the other. I believe that if I have another drink, it will do me no harm." So she took another hearty drink, and sent the second chicken running after the first one. Just as she was making the most of it, her master returned, calling out, "Gretel, hurry up, the guest is right behind me." "Yes, sir, I'm getting it ready," answered Gretel. Meanwhile the master saw that the table was set, and he picked up the large knife that he wanted to carve the chickens with, and stood in the hallway sharpening it. The guest arrived and knocked politely on the door. Gretel ran to see who it was, and when she saw that it was the guest, she held a finger before her mouth, and said, "Be quiet! Be quiet! Hurry and get away from here. If my master catches you, you'll be sorry. Yes, he invited you for an evening meal, but all he really wants is to cut off both of your ears. Listen, he's sharpening his knife for it right now." The guest heard the whetting and ran back down the steps as fast as he could. Then Gretel, who was not a bit lazy, ran to her master, crying, "Just what kind of a guest did you invite?" "Why, Gretel? What do you mean by that?" "Well," she said, "he took both of the chickens off the platter, just as I was about to carry them out, and then ran away with them."

Tale #077; **Clever Gretel**

Intent: To manipulate a situation in order to keep from getting caught for wrongdoings you have committed- which another is just as guilty of doing themselves.
Timing: The dark of the moon

Materials:

Chicken pieces	Small potatoes	Cooking materials
Rosemary	Salt and pepper	Wine of choice

This spell will require at least rudimentary cooking skills as it is a kitchen spell.

Start by peeling the potatoes and carving them into the shape of an ear; you may go as detailed as it pleases you, but small potatoes (such as Red Potatoes or baby varieties) are best for this. When they are finished, coat them generously in Salt, Pepper, and Olive Oil. Add a bit of crushed Rosemary, then toss well. Bake in the oven at 350 degrees Fahrenheit (175 degrees Celsius) until they are just tender enough to allow a fork to go through easily, but not so tender as they crumble apart completely.

In a high rimmed cooking pan, bring together 1 cup of a wine of your choice (preferably one that goes well with Rosemary and Chicken) with salt, and pepper to taste. Allow it to come to a boil, then reduce the heat to low. Place the chicken in the pan (Chicken Wings are best, but you may use boneless skinless chicken breast if you desire), and allow it to simmer until cooked with the lid off to allow for evaporation.

If you time this correctly, both the potatoes and chicken should be finished at roughly the same time. Remove them, and make two small plates so that they equal a single portion when combined. Pour yourself a glass of the same wine you used to cook, then sit down at your table and consume the first plate in silence.

Once you have finished the first plate, hold your hands over the second and say:

What is right for one cannot be wrong for another
And yet to you I will have done no harm

Consume the second plate in silence again and the spell is complete.

Little Nettle Plant

When the night came, and the bridge was to be led into the Prince's apartment, [the serving maid] let he veil fall over her face, that he might not observe the deception. As soon as everyone had gone away, he said to her, "What didst thou say to the nettle-plant which was growing by the wayside?" [...] She went out and sought Maid Maleen. "Girl, what hast thou been saying to the nettle?" "I said nothing but 'Oh, nettle-plant, Little nettle-plant, What dost thou here alone? I have known the time When I ate thee unboiled, When I ate thee unroasted.' "

Tale #198; Maid Maleen

Intent: To break another's glamour or remove a disguise.
Timing: Waning or waxing moon

Materials:

Shallow bowl	Small sauce pot	Straining material
	Photo of target	
Vetiver and Mustard Seed, plus 3 fresh stalks or 3 tbsp of dried Nettle		

Gather three stalks of nettles; for those of us who don't want our hands stung to pieces, three large spoonfuls of dried Nettle will do. Add to this one spoonful of Vetiver and one small pinch of Mustard Seeds. Simmer the herbs in about three cups of water for 10 minutes, then strain the infusion through coffee filters or cheesecloth to remove the plant material. If you wish to skip straining altogether, simply sew the herbs up into a coffee filter and toss that into the water instead.

Acquire an image of the target, or write their full name on a slip of paper. Cut or tear this into small pieces and place the pieces in a shallow bowl. Carefully pour the strained infusion into the bowl until all the pieces are soaked and submerged. Don't put too much water in the bowl; just enough to cover the paper will do.

Position the bowl so that the sun's light is reflected in the water and leave it out until all the water has evaporated. As the water steams away, the target's glamour goes with it. Once the water is gone, take the paper pieces and discard them as you would any garbage.

Spell Creation Worksheet

Title of Tale: _____

Inspirational Passage: _____
_____
_____
_____

Nature: _____ **Intent:** _____ **Target:** _____

Duration and Timing: _____

Materials: _____
_____
_____

Casting Method: _____

Instructions: _____
_____
_____
_____
_____
_____
_____
_____

Notes: _____
_____

Spell Creation Worksheet

Title of Tale: _____

Inspirational Passage: _____
_____
_____
_____

Nature: _____ **Intent:** _____ **Target:** _____

Duration and Timing: _____

Materials: _____
_____
_____

Casting Method: _____

Instructions: _____
_____
_____
_____
_____
_____
_____
_____
_____

Notes: _____
_____

Spell Creation Worksheet

Title of Tale: _____

Inspirational Passage: _____
_____
_____
_____
_____

Nature: _____ **Intent:** _____ **Target:** _____

Duration and Timing: _____

Materials: _____
_____
_____
_____

Casting Method: _____

Instructions: _____
_____
_____
_____
_____
_____
_____
_____
_____
_____

Notes: _____
_____

Spell Creation Worksheet

Title of Tale: _____

Inspirational Passage: _____
_____
_____
_____
_____

Nature: _____ **Intent:** _____ **Target:** _____

Duration and Timing: _____

Materials: _____
_____
_____

Casting Method: _____

Instructions: _____
_____
_____
_____
_____
_____
_____
_____
_____

Notes: _____
_____

Revelation and Truth Seeking

When all is said and done, the act of revealing things covers a wide variety of subjects. The most common revelatory themes in Faery Tales, however, are twofold: The act of divining the future, and the revealing of truth in a situation where one has potentially been misled or lied to. Another theme that is common- though a bit less so- is the revelation of which path or direction to take, or that of a solution to a problem faced.

We are of the opinion that the most beneficial and least depressing of these themes is that of the direction or solution. This is because there are many faults in other areas of revelation- though this, like much else, is not to say that we disagree with their usage. However, we do still recognize these failures and complications as things to be acknowledged when practicing magic.

The first is that there are several opinions on whether future telling is possible. Many believe that the future is not set in stone; that it is changeable depending on your actions leading up to the point you are trying to foresee. This leads to the idea that you can know the future, but that the future you know may not be the one to eventually occur. You cannot tell whether changing your actions will necessarily affect its outcome, but it is believed by some that once you know the future it may not come true due to a probable subconscious change in demeanor and action on the person's part to either help or prevent that future from coming to fruition. On the other side of the spectrum, others believe that the future is impossible to know altogether for one reason or another.

Likewise, truth-seeking may not give the clearest or most accurate explanations of an event that you are seeking revelation of. It can, however, help to reveal a simple answer or help you determine whether further action is needed. The truth is often not always a pretty thing, as well. Indeed, the truth can oftentimes be far worse than the lies you are prospectively facing. Whatever the truth or future you are seeking to reveal, know this and be prepared to deal with it- and when it is revealed to you, accept it.

It stands to reason, then, that divination and truth seeking is a rather nebulous area of magic- though one which can still be rewarding to the practitioner.

Three Twigs In A Teacup

Then they went all the down [the steps], and when they were at the bottom, they were standing in a wonderfully pretty avenue of trees, all of the leaves of which were of silver, and shone and glistened. The soldier thought, "I must carry a token away with me," and broke off a twig from one of them.. After that, they came into an avenue where the leaves were all of gold, and lastly into a third avenue where they were of bright diamonds. He broke off a piece from each. The third time he took a cup away with him as a token. When the hour arrived for him to give his answer, he took the three twigs and the cup, and went to the King, but the twelve [princesses] stood behind the door, and listened for what he was going to say. When the King put the question, "Where have my twelve daughters danced their shoes to pieces in the night?" he answered, "In an underground castle with the twelve Princes," and related how it had come to pass, and brought out the tokens.

Tale #133; **The Shoes That Were Danced to Pieces**

Intent: To determine the answer to a simple question through divination.
Ideal Timing: This spell can be performed anytime.

Materials:

Teacup or Mug	Three Twigs	Pitcher of water
Waterproof paint in Silver, White, and Gold		

To answer simple questions, find a fair-sized teacup and gather three twigs of equal length which are small enough to fit inside it horizontally. Paint each twig an individual color (one silver, one gold, and one white); if you prefer other colors, feel free to use them so long as the paint is waterproof and you can easily tell the three twigs apart. Make sure that the twigs will float in water once the paint is dry.

To use the twigs and teacup for divination, place the three twigs in the cup, standing on end- though it is fine if they lean against the sides of the cup. Hold a question in your mind or ask it aloud as you slowly fill the cup with water; it is best to use a teapot or a pitcher for the pouring rather than a faucet so that the sticks float up naturally.

Watch for one of the sticks to float up and fall out of the cup. If the silver twig falls first, the answer is "No" or "Not at this time". If the golden twig falls first, the answer is "Yes" or "It will come to be". If the white twig falls first, the answer is "It is not clear" or "More must come to pass". You can also assign your own divinatory meanings to each twig for more complex questions.

Be sure to dry the twigs between divinations and before storage to prevent molding and breakage.

The Poisoned Comb

And by witchcraft she made a poisoned comb. Then she dressed herself up to look like another different sort of old woman. So she went across the seven mountains and came to the house of the seven dwarfs, and knocked at the door and cried, "Good wares to sell! good wares to sell!" Snow-white looked out and said, "Go away, I must not let anybody in." "But you are not forbidden to look," said the old woman, taking out the poisoned comb and holding it up. It pleased the poor child so much that she was tempted to open the door.

Tale #053; **Little Snow-White**

Intent: To reveal deception.
Ideal Timing: This spell can be performed anytime.

Materials:

A single Violet flower	Metal comb or fork	White or black candle

For this spell, you will need the type of metal comb that holds hair in place- not a comb meant for detangling one's hair. If you cannot find a metal comb, a fork will do in a pinch.

Whisper the name of the person you believe is deceiving you to the violet, then spear the blossom with the teeth of the comb and hold it over the flame of the candle.

If the flower burns slowly, curling in on itself, there is no deception. However, if the flower burns quickly, in a bright flash, the named party is lying to you about something and you should make it your business to find out what.

The Singing Bone

As soon as the flock passed over the bridge, [the herdsman] waded into the middle of the stream - for the water was very shallow - took up the bone, and carried it home to make a mouthpiece for his horn. But the first time he blew the horn after the bone was in it, it filled the herdsman with wonder and amazement; for it began to sing of itself, and these were the words it sang: "Ah! dear shepherd, you are blowing your horn With one of my bones, which night and morn Lie still unburied, beneath the wave Where I was thrown in a sandy grave. I killed the wild boar, and my brother slew me, And gained the Princess by pretending 'twas he."

Tale #028; The Singing Bone

Intent: To reveal the misdeeds of another.
Ideal Timing: Waxing or Full Moon

Materials:

Small flute or whistle	Photo of the target	Black candle

Obtain a small wind instrument of any type; if you cannot obtain one then any blown instrument which produces a high, clear sound will do. If it happens to be white, that is a bonus but it is not a requirement.

For targeting, you may use a photograph of the person or their name on a piece of paper. Set light to a black chime candle and think of the misdeed which you want brought to light and the attention of others. Say three times:

> *Though hidden is your treachery,*
> *My flute of bone shall sing to thee,*
> *And all the world the truth shall see.*

After each recitation, blow a long note on your instrument or play a brief tune. Each time, drip three drops of wax onto the photo or name slip. When you have finished, burn the name slip or photo in a fire-safe dish, then let the candle burn down completely.

The Bird's Warning

So she went on the whole day until she came to the middle of the wood, where it was darkest, and there stood a lonely house, not pleasant in her eyes, for it was dismal and unhomelike. She walked in, but there was no one there, and the greatest stillness reigned. Suddenly she heard a voice cry, "Turn back, turn back, thou pretty bride, within this house thou must not bide, for here do evil things betide." The girl glanced around, and perceived that the voice came from a bird who was hanging in a cage by the wall. And again it cried, "Turn back, turn back, thou pretty bride, within this house thou must not bide, for here do evil things betide."

Tale #040; The Robber Bridegroom

Intent: To warn someone of imminent danger that they will not, or cannot, see.
Ideal Timing: Full Moon, but this charm can be made anytime.

Materials:

Craft feathers	Glue	Cardboard
Scissors	A small cloth bag	A heavy, flat object
Paint or markers	Bells x3	White thread or yarn
	Rosemary and Bay Leaf	

Acquire some craft feathers. The color and type do not matter so long as they will stand up to being worked with. If you wish to include color magic in your charm, however, I suggest any of the following: Yellow for clarity and persuasion, Orange for courage and victory. Red for strength and swift action, or White for passive protection

Cut two small half-moon shapes out of the cardboard, about 2" (5cm) across. Glue shaft ends of the feathers to one of the cutouts to create a fan shape. Work in layers with the longest feathers on the bottom and the shortest ones on top until you have a pretty solid-looking fan; it may help to lay the feathers out first, then set them in place on the cardboard.

Next cut a small loop of strong thread or yarn and place the ends in the center of the flat side of the cardboard piece. This will be your hanging loop, so make sure there's enough to hold the piece up. Glue the other cardboard piece on top to sandwich the feathers and loop in place, then carefully lay a heavy flat object- like a book or paperweight- over the cardboard pieces to press them flat. Do not compress the feathers if you can help it, but leave the piece to dry on a flat surface overnight.

The next day you can paint the cardboard however you wish, with a solid color or some design that matches the feathers in the fan. When you are finished, carefully sew a trio of jingle bells to the feathers just beneath the cardboard. This will be the front of your fan. Afterwards place the rosemary and bay leaf in the cloth bag and stitch this to the back of the fan, on the opposite side from the jingle bells. The bag should be small enough that the feathers cover it when the fan is viewed from the front.

Once the fan is complete, gift it to the person who needs to be warned of danger. The magic will work best if the person willingly accepts the gift. If all else fails, you can bind their name or image to the charm and put it in a safe place in your own home.

The Three Ravens

It happened, however, as they were still journeying on the open sea, that Faithful John, as he sat in the forepart of the ship and made music, caught sight of three ravens in the air flying overhead. Then he stopped playing, and listened to what they said one to another, for he understood them quite well. The first one cried, " Ay, there goes the Princess of the Golden Palace." "Yes" answered the second "but he has not got her safe yet."

Tale #006; **Faithful Johannes**

Intent: To create a charm that will warn of impending danger.
Ideal Timing: This charm can be created anytime.

Materials:

1 yard of White yarn	1 yard of Black yarn	1 yard of Red yarn
Black craft feathers x9		Bells

This particular charm is bound up in an item called a Witches' Ladder. Prepare three 1-yard (1m) strands of yarn. Traditional colors for witches' ladders are red, black, and white, but the colors can be anything you like. You can also include multiple strands, so long as the number is a multiple of 2 or 3 depending on whether you want to tie knots or make a braid.

Braid or knot the strands together. At regular intervals, attach a feather and a bell. Use a dot of glue to help secure the feathers if you need to. As you braid or tie knots, focus on the intention of the spell. Chant as you work:

> *Ravens circling in the sky,*
> *Keep all harm and hurt at bay.*
> *If some evil you should spy,*
> *Warn me if it comes my way.*
> *In this ladder your warning dwells.*
> *Flap your wings and ring the bells.*

Once the ladder is complete, tie three more bells to the bottom of the strand.

Hang the ladder somewhere that it will not be disturbed by breezes from air ducts, doors, windows, or people passing by it. When the bells should ring when not stirred by mundane causes, beef up your protections and beware of trouble of danger headed your way.

Three Golden Hairs

"...I dreamed of a wall in a market-place from which wine once used to flow, but now it is dried up, and they can't even get water from it. Whose fault is that?" "Ah, they ought to know that there sits a toad under a stone in the well, and if he were dead, wine would again flow." "I dreamed that in a certain country there grows a fruit tree which used to bear golden apples, but now it produces nothing but leaves. What is the cause of this"? "Why, don't they know that there is a mouse gnawing at the root? Were it dead, the tree would again bear golden apples; and if it gnaws much longer the tree will wither and dry up." "I dreamed about a ferryman, who complains that he is obliged to take people across the river, and is never free." "Oh, the stupid fellow! He can very easily ask any person who wants to be ferried over to take the oar in his hand, and he will be free at once."

Tale #029; **The Devil with the Three Golden Hairs**

Intent: To discover the solution to a difficult problem.
Ideal Timing: Waxing, Waning, or Full Moon

Materials:

| Gold embroidery floss x3 | Paper | Writing utensil |

On a small slip of paper, write down the problem that's plaguing you and what you believe might be standing in the way of a solution. Fold up the paper and set it aside.

Acquire some golden embroidery floss or fine yarn. Cut three strands of equal length and carefully braid them to together. As you do, focus on the on the problem which needs solving.

Once the braid is finished, wrap it around the folded paper and tie it loosely. Hang the bundle in the window for a day and a night, then tuck the paper away and tie the braid around your wrist or ankle. Wear it until it falls off naturally or a solution to your problem presents itself, whichever comes first.

Mirror of Truth

He entered and went through all the rooms, until in the last he found the King's daughter. But how shocked he was when he saw her. She had an ashen-grey face full of wrinkles, bleary eyes, and red hair. "Art thou the King's daughter, whose beauty the whole world praises?" said he. "Ah," she answered, "this is not my form; human eyes can only see me in this state of ugliness, but that thou mayst know what I am like, look in the mirror - it does not let itself be misled - it will show thee my image as it is in truth."

Tale #197; **The Crystal Ball**

Intent: To clear away deception and show someone for who they truly are.
Ideal Timing: Waxing Moon, for revelation and an increase in perception

Materials:

Photo of the target	Small Mirror	Paper
Black yarn or ribbon		Black cloth bag

Obtain a photo of the target and bind it to a small mirror so that the back of the photo faces out. Symbolically, the target is now looking into and appearing in the mirror. Hold the photo and mirror between your hands and say:

> *Lovely as grace or ugly as sin*
> *The inside's out, the outside's in.*
> *The mirror's glass your true face will show,*
> *And you and I alone will know**

Wrap the photo and the mirror with paper and bind it up with black yarn or ribbon to hold everything in place. Repeat the incantation as you do so, to give the spell additional strength. Once the packet is entirely wrapped, place it into a black cloth bag and tuck it away.

Watch the target carefully over the next few days. If they are being deceptive, you should start to notice where their promises ring false, where their expressions are hollow, or where their stories have holes in them. Alternatively, you may discover something truly lovely about the person that they have kept hidden for reasons of their own.

*If you wish for wider or more public revelation, replace the last line in the incantation with, "And may all who look upon you know". Either way, the person will be revealed to you for who they truly are- for better or worse. What you do with that knowledge is up to you.

Pennies in the Sun

Then he told her how years ago, when he was traveling about seeking work and quite worn out and penniless, he had killed a [man], and that in the last agonies of death, the [man] had spoken the words, "The bright sun will bring it to light." And now, the sun had just wanted to bring it to light, and had gleamed and made circles on the wall, but had not been able to do it. After this, he again charged her particularly never to tell this, or he would lose his life, and she did promise. When, however, he had sat down to work again, she went to her great friend and confided the story to her, but she was never to repeat it to any human being, but before two days were over, the whole town knew it, and the tailor was brought to trial, and condemned. And thus, after all, the bright sun did bring it to light.

Tale #115; **The Bright Sun Will Bring It to Light**

Intent: To bring hidden truth to light.
Ideal Timing: Around the Full Moon for discernment, but can be performed anytime.

Materials:

Shiny pennies x8

For this spell, all you need are eight shiny pennies. If you can only get your hands on dull, tarnished ones, you can clean them by mixing 1/4 cup White Vinegar and 1 tsp Salt in a ceramic or plastic bowl (the bowl MUST be non-metal, that's very important), stirring it well with a non-metal utensil until the salt dissolves, adding the pennies waiting about 10 seconds. Take them from the solution, then, rinse them well with water, and buff them with a paper towel.

Place the bright, shiny pennies in a window where the sun will shine upon them. Leave them there undisturbed for three days- then spend them, give them, or leave them where you wish to find discernment or where some hidden truth needs to be brought to light.

Little Grey String

The master now believed that he would be safe for the third night, and he lay down in his own bed. This time the princess herself came. She had on a mist-gray robe and sat down next to him. When she thought that he was asleep and dreaming, she spoke to him, hoping that he would answer in his sleep, like many do. However, he was still awake and understood and heard everything very well. Then she asked, "One killed none. What is that?" He answered, "A raven that ate from a dead and poisoned horse, and died of it." She asked further, "But still killed twelve. What is that?" He answered, "Those are twelve murderers who ate the raven and died of it". Now that she knew the riddle she wanted to sneak away[...] The next morning, the princess announced that she had guessed the riddle and sent for the twelve judges and solved it before them.

Tale #022; **The Riddle**

Intent: To reveal an answer to something you need help with or cannot find the answer to.
Ideal Timing: This spell can be performed anytime, but a full moon is best for light.

Materials:

Salt		Water
Grey, White, Yellow, and Pale Blue Yarn or Thread		

Ideally, the colors of yarn used should be grey, white, yellow, and pale blue. If these are not available, use all grey yarn instead.

With the 4 threads or strings of yarn, weave a bracelet using a simple macrame or friendship bracelet technique. While braiding, recite:

One for help, and Two for a plea
Three for an answer, and Four to see

When finished, combine the salt with the water and soak the bracelet in it overnight in the light of the moon. The next day, take it out, and allow it to air dry.

Wear the bracelet any time you are having trouble studying, when you are taking tests, when you need help making a decision or seeing which path you should take, or any other instance which you need an answer revealed to you.

The Golden Ball

The frog, as soon as he heard her promise, drew his head under the water and sank down out of sight, but after a while he came to the surface again with the ball in his mouth, and he threw it on the grass. The King's daughter was overjoyed to see her pretty plaything again, and she caught it up and ran off with it.

Tale #001; **The Frog King**

Intent: To find and retrieve a lost object.
Ideal Timing: This spell can be cast whenever needed.

Materials:

| Bowl of water | A gold or yellow marble | Tea ball on a chain |

If you cannot find a gold or yellow marble then use a waterproof paint on one of any color. Allow the paint to dry before continuing.

Fill a deep bowl about three quarters of the way with water to represent the pond. Place the gold marble or ball bearing into the tea ball, then hold the tea ball between your hands. Picture the item that you're trying to find. Drop the tea ball into the bowl and let it sink to the bottom.

Peer into the surface of the water, letting your eyes go unfocused, and say three times:

Marble golden, marble round
From your hiding place rebound
What is lost, let now be found

After the third recitation, pull the chain and bring up the tea ball. Take out the marble and hold it in your fist, then hold that hand out before you and see if you feel a pull toward any particular location. It may not be a physical pull, so be aware of nudges or sudden ideas of where to look.

Baneful Magics

The realm of Faery Tales is rife with instances of Baneful Magics being performed for one reason or another. Some people, however, will nonetheless disagree with our decision to include a chapter on Baneful Magics in this book. This form of magic is ultimately the most controversial within the community and is subject to much debate; there is a wide range of opinions on the subject and whether or not a person should or should not include it in their practice.

Ultimately, both of us are of the personal mindset that Baneful Magics can be positive, helpful things when necessary despite their often negative nature. This is the primary reason why we have elected to include them.

A question that Bree is asked quite regularly on this topic is some variation of "How do I protect myself from the backlash of casting baneful magic / perform cursing without consequences?". As she has so often said, "You can't sling mud without getting your hands dirty"- but just like with mud, there are things you can do to mitigate the mess.

Considering the possible outcomes, closing as many loopholes as you can before casting so that you wind up with less of a chance of an unfavorable result, as well as shielding yourself (see: Don Thy Armor) before you perform baneful magic, and cleansing afterwards (see: The Seven Year Bath), will often minimize the risk of getting bashed in the teeth if the spell rebounds or goes awry.

But even if you do everything suggested here, that doesn't necessarily mean you won't have to pay a price, or that your spell will not have some form of rebound. In our experiences this price is often the energy of the caster required to fuel the spell, but it is normally nothing that a square meal and good night's rest won't solve. With baneful spells, the effect or price you pay can sometimes be more severe, because of the intent of the magic involved.

Much like throwing a punch, we don't recommend that baneful magic be your first response to troubling or hurtful situations. Because much like throwing a punch, it has the potential to feel good in the moment, but subsequently make things worse than they were before. Try the 24-Hour Rule - If you're still angry enough to sling a curse after you've slept on the thought of it, then go ahead and stuff that poppet or make that jar.

It's important to note that failed spells generally do not have the same backlash that baneful magics do. A spell that fizzles out or just does not work for whatever reason usually has a minimum of danger to the caster, much like a missed shot in basketball. But then there are still times when the ball bounces off the rim and smacks you in the face.

Curses are much more potent and therefore carry a greater risk. It does not automatically mean that someone is going to drop a house on you, but the price can range from just having a couple of bad days to full on backlash where the curse you threw boomerangs around and bites you square on the rump. Whatever you choose to do, you need to accept that there is a price to cursing, just like with any other magic. Regardless of how and when it manifests, the simple truth is that performing baneful magic without incurring consequences is ultimately impossible and there is no getting out of paying up. If you are uncomfortable with that, then the suggestion is to find another way to get things done; if you do not want the hassle, then ultimately you should not be performing this particular type of magic.

Bite My Shiny Red Apple

"Are you afraid of poison?" said the woman, "look here, I will cut the apple in two pieces; you shall have the red side, I will have the white one." For the apple was so cunningly made, that all the poison was in the rosy half of it. Snow White longed for the beautiful apple, and as she saw the peasant woman eating a piece of it she could no longer refrain, but stretched out her hand and took the poisoned half. But no sooner had she taken a morsel of it into her mouth than she fell to the earth as dead.

Tale #053; **Little Snow-White**

Intent: To remove or banish troublesome persons from your home.
Ideal Timing: Waning Moon

Materials:

A red apple	Paring knife or peeler	Cutting knife

Take a rosy red apple and polish it until it shines. Carefully peel half of it to reveal the white flesh beneath. Cut the apple in half so that the red is on one side and the white on the other. Carve the target's name into the red half; eat the white half yourself.

Take the red half outside and either cast it far away from your home or leave it where it will be devoured by local wildlife.

Or, if you're very clever, you can bake the carved half of the apple into a small pie or tartlet and give it to the target to eat. Do not, however, do not do anything to the food that would cause physical harm or illness. This is banishing, not manslaughter.

Into the Oven

The witch pushed poor Gretel toward the oven, out of which the flames were already shining. "Creep in," said the witch, "and see if it is properly hot, so that the bread may be baked." And Gretel once in, she meant to shut the door upon her. But Gretel perceived her intention, and said, "I don't know how to do it; how shall I get in?" "Stupid goose," said the old woman, "the opening is big enough, do you see? I could get in myself!" And she stooped down and put her head in the oven's mouth. Then Gretel gave her a push, so that she went in farther, and she shut the iron door upon her, and put up the bar. Oh how frightfully she howled! But Gretel ran away, and left the wicked witch to burn miserably.

Tale #015; **Hansel and Gretel.**

Intent: To trap and punish those who mean you harm.
Ideal Timing: Waning or Dark of the Moon, but can be performed any time

Materials:

Cookie dough	Person-shaped cookie cutter	Baking sheets

Roll out some gingerbread or sugar cookie dough into a flat sheet. You can make the dough from scratch or use premade, both are equally viable. With a cookie-cutter, cut out one person-shaped cookie for every person you believe means you active harm. Carefully place the cookies on a prepared baking sheet. Just before you pop them in to bake, say over the cookie poppets:

You mean to harm me, this I know
The oven is open, so in you go!

Bake the cookies according to the recipe or package directions. You can decorate them with frosting when they're done if you wish, then sit back with a glass of milk and enjoy the satisfaction of biting the heads off of your enemies.

Logs In The Fire

"Ah, for once it burns brightly!"

Tale Number Unknown; **The Old Witch**

Intent: To curse people who refuse to mind their own business.
Ideal Timing: Dark of the moon, but can be performed anytime.

Materials:

| A piece of wood | Carving or writing implement | Fire safe burning place |

For this spell, you will need a wood-burning fireplace, a bonfire, a campfire, or a fire safe bowl of sufficient size to burn the material. Always exercise common sense and fire safety when performing this type of magic.

Find a thick stick or small block of wood the length of your hand. Carve into or write upon it the name of the person who insists on interfering with your business.

Toss the wood into the fire, saying:

Keep your nose to youself,
Or else let it be burnt!

Let the wood burn to ash, then scatter it in a strong wind.

Bellyful of Stones

When the wolf at length had had his sleep out, he got on his legs, and as the stones in his stomach made him very thirsty, he wanted to go to a well to drink. But when he began to walk and to move about, the stones in his stomach knocked against each other and rattled. Then cried he "What rumbles and tumbles Against my poor bone? I thought 'twas six kids but it's naught but big stones." And when he got to the well and stooped over the water and was just about to drink, the heavy stones made him fall in and there was no help, but he had to drown miserably.

Tale #005; The Wolf and the Seven Young Kids

Intent: To turn harm back upon a person whose greed is causing strife.
Ideal Timing: Waning or Dark of the Moon.

Materials:

Poppet	Material focus	Scissors
Needle and thread	Small stones x7	Thumbtacks or thorns x7
A Whole Chili Pepper		

Make or acquire a cloth poppet. You're going to be stuffing the poppet, so make sure it's a decent size, with plenty of room in the stomach area. It is not necessary to have any hair or nails from the target in order to make the spell work, but it can help. In the absence of such things, you can name the poppet to represent them.

With scissors or a small sharp blade, open a slit in the belly of the poppet. If there is pre-existing filling, remove some of it. Into the cavity where the stomach might be, place a whole chili pepper (any kind will do), seven small pebbles, and seven tacks or thorns. Carefully stitch the poppet closed and whisper to it:

> *Rumble and tumble,*
> *A pepper and stones.*
> *Swallow your greed,*
> *And choke on the bones.*

Take the poppet to a deep body of water, such as a lake or pond, and drop it into the deepest part you can reach. If such a body of water is not available, you can "drown" the poppet in a bucket of water for three nights and then discard it with your garbage.

Mouthful of Flames

When he had gone away, she ordered a young hind to be brought and killed; then she cut out its heart and its tongue, and put them on a dish. When she saw the old man coming she said to the boy, "Get into bed, and cover yourself right over." The old scoundrel came in and said, "Where are the tongue and the heart of the boy?" The maiden gave him the dish, but the Prince threw off the coverings, and said, "You old sinner, why did you want to kill me? Now bear your sentence. You shall be turned into a black poodle, with a gold chain round your neck, and you shall be made to eat live coals, so that flames of fire may come out of your mouth."

Tale #076; The Pink

Intent: To punish one who meant to do you harm or who has slandered you.
Ideal Timing: Dark of the Moon

Materials:

Matches x3	Newspaper	Trowel
Garden pot	Potting soil	A knife
Paper		Writing utensil
A Bell Pepper of any color, and Small Hot Peppers- also of any color		

Acquire a small bell pepper. The color doesn't particularly matter, so feel free to pick whatever's cheapest. On the same trip, pick up a few smaller chili peppers. They can be any type you want, fresh or dried, as long as they're hot.

With a small paring knife, carefully remove the stem and seed core of the bell pepper. If you like, you can remove the seeds from the core and set them on a paper towel to dry overnight. These can be useful in future spellwork. Slice the chili peppers into pieces small enough to fit inside the bell pepper. You can save the seeds from these as well.

Prepare a slip of paper with the name of the target. Spoon pieces of chopped chilies into the bell pepper until it is half filled. Add the name slip. Then strike three matches, one after the other, blow them out, and drop them in. With each match, say:

Whenever you choose to let your tongue slip,
May flames of fire burn in your lips.

For a more potent curse, add more matches, in multiples of three. Fill the rest of the bell pepper with chopped chilies, then wrap the whole thing in a sheet of newsprint. Bury the wrapped pepper in a garden or planter pot and leave it to decompose.

Out of the Sack

When bedtime came the guest stretched himself on a bench, and put his sack under his head for a pillow, and the landlord, when he thought the young man was sound asleep, came, and, stooping down, pulled gently at the sack, so as to remove it cautiously, and put another in its place. The turner has only been waiting for this to happen, and just as the landlord was giving a last courageous pull, he cried, "Stick, out of the sack!" Out flew the stick directly, and laid to heartily on the landlord's back; and in vain he begged for mercy; the louder he cried the harder the stick beat time on his back, until he fell exhausted to the ground. Then the turner said, "If you do not give me the table and the ass directly, this game shall begin all over again." "Oh dear, no!" cried the landlord, quite collapsed; "I will gladly give it all back again is you will only make this terrible goblin go back into the sack." Then said the young man, "I will be generous instead of just, but beware!" Then he cried, "Stick, into the sack!" and left him in peace.

Tale #036; **Table-be-Set, Gold-Donkey, and Cudgel-out-of-the-Sack**

Intent: To punish one who has stolen from you.
Ideal Timing: This spell can be performed anytime.

Materials:

Poppet	Hazel stick	Needle
Sewing thread	Material focus	Cloth bag
Elder Berry and Willow Bark		

Acquire a twig from a hazel tree. It should be small but sturdy and not easy to break. If possible, take one that has broken off and fallen to the ground naturally. If you must pick one from a living tree, give the tree some water and say thank you, and don't take more than you absolutely need. It's only polite.

Make or obtain a cloth poppet. Open the torso and stuff the poppet's chest with a spoonful of dried Elder Berries and another of Willow Bark. Add the material focus last, then carefully sew the poppet closed with the herbs inside. If there is no material focus then simply name the poppet in order to represent them; if the thief is unknown, simply name it "Thief".

Give the poppet a good thrashing with the hazel stick once a day for three to seven days. In the case of an unknown thief, seven days should be enough. If you know the person who has stolen from you, continue until they are caught or confess. If they steal from you again, repeat the spell until they've learned their lesson.

The Bottle Trap

"Knowest thou," [the spirit] cried in an awful voice, "what thy wages are for having let me out?" "No," replied the scholar fearlessly, "how should I know that?" "Then I will tell thee," cried the spirit; "I must strangle thee for it" [...] "Softly," answered the scholar, "not so fast. I must first know that thou wert shut up in that little bottle, and that thou art the right spirit. If, indeed, thou canst get in again, I will believe, and then thou mayst do as thou wilt with me." The spirit said haughtily, "That is a very trifling feat," drew himself together, and made himself as small and slender as he had been at first, so that he crept through the same opening, and right through the neck of the bottle again. Scarcely was he within than the scholar thrust the cork he had drawn back into the bottle, and threw it among the roots of the oak into its old place, and the spirit was betrayed.

Tale #099; **The Spirit in the Glass Bottle**

Intent: To entrap an enemy and punish them with confusion.
Ideal Timing: Dark Moon, but this charm can be made anytime.

Materials:

Glass jar with screw lid	Glitter glue	Small glass marble
1 Cup hot water	Sequins	Water-tight tape
Room temperature water	Food coloring	Loose glitter

Choose a glass marble to represent the person you wish to entrap. A dark color like silver, cobalt blue, or black will work best, but the marble can be any color you like as long as it's small. You don't want something heavy banging around inside your jar which might cause damage. Hold the marble and charm it thus:

Down side up and outside in,
I'll send your world into a spin.
Inside out and upside down,
I'll turn your smiles into frowns.
[Name], my curse upon your head,
Let all your joy be pain instead.

Pour 1 cup of hot water into your chosen container. Squeeze in about 2 tablespoons of glitter glue and carefully stir the solution with a small whisk or a fork until the glue dissolves. Add glitter and sequins to the container. Depending on the size of the container, you'll want about 1/2" of glittery material in the bottom. If you wish to add color to the water, you can put in a drop or two of food coloring in the hue of your choice but don't use too much, or the water will turn opaque. A little food coloring goes a long way!

At this point, you should put in the bespelled glass marble. Then fill the container the rest of the way with room-temperature water, leaving a little space at the top for shaking. Screw the lid on and secure it with duct tape or electrical tape to prevent leaks.

Whenever the person gives you grief, or you just want to mess with their day, shake the container and watch the marble fly through the shimmery water with no hope of escape.

Wicked Thorns

Then [the witch] let down the hair, and the King's son climbed up, but instead of his dearest Rapunzel, he found the witch looking at him with wicked, glittering eyes. "Aha!" cried she, mocking him, "you came for your darling, but the sweet bird sits no longer in the nest, and sings no more; the cat has got her, and will scratch out your eyes as well! Rapunzel is lost to you, you will see her no more." The King's son was beside himself with grief, and in his agony he sprang from the tower; he escaped with life, but the thorns on which he fell put out his eyes.

Tale #012; Rapunzel

Intent: To (figuratively, not literally) blind your enemies to your movements and actions.
Ideal Timing: Dark or Waning Moon

Materials:

Poppet	Swatch of black cloth	Thorns or thumbtacks

Create a poppet from cloth or clay. If you have a bit of hair or a nail clipping from the target, add that as well. If not, you can name the poppet to represent them.

Press the thorns or thumbtacks into the spots where the eyes would be. Don't bother being gentle about it, but be careful not to prick your own fingers in the process. As you do, say three times:

Deepest water, blackest night
I blind your eyes, I take your sight

Wrap the poppet in the black cloth, being sure to cover the head, and place it in a shoebox until such time as you no longer require its' services.

To remove the spell, retrieve the box and unwrap the poppet. Remove the thorns and the focus- if there is one- and burn them. The poppet can be burned as well, or you can bury it in salt to negate lingering magic.

Drop the Millstone

Just as she came to the door, crash went the millstone on her head, and crushed her flat.

Tale #047; **The Juniper Tree**

Intent: To take revenge upon someone who has done you grievous wrong.
Ideal Timing: Dark of the Moon,

Materials:

Poppet	Material Focus	Juniper sprigs or berries
Newspaper	Thick string or yarn	Smooth round stone

Make a simple clay poppet. For this particular spell, a clay poppet is important. The poppet can be made from commercially-available modeling clay or you can make an easy salt dough recipe. Include a bit of hair or a nail clipping from your target as a focus. If these things are not available, you can name the poppet to represent the target.

Press juniper berries or sprigs of juniper into the clay, excluding the head. As you do so, think of the wrongs this person has done to you. You can even count them on the berries and sprigs if you like. Take a smooth round stone with a decent amount of weight to it and hold it over the poppet's head. Speak over the stone:

By the millstone in my hand
Your hold on me is at an end
On your own head be it!

Drop the stone so that it squashes the poppet's head, then wrap the stone and the squashed poppet together with some newspaper. Tie it securely and drop the bundle into a body of water deep enough that the stone can't be seen from the surface; alternatively you can drop it into a hole with similar properties or the stone bundle may also be buried if you wish.

Three Beatings A Day

After the huntsman had washed his face, so that the transformed ones could recognize him, he went down into the courtyard, and said, "Now you shall receive the wages of your treachery!" and bound them together, all three with one rope, and drove them along until he came to a mill. He knocked at the window, the miller put out his head, and asked what we wanted. "I have three unmanageable beasts," answered he, "which I don't want to keep any longer. Will you take them in, and give them food and stable room, and manage them as I tell you, and then I will pay you what you ask." The miller said, "Why not? But how am I to manage them?" The huntsman then said that he was to give three beatings and one meal daily to the old donkey, and that was the witch; one beating and three meals to the younger one, which was the servant-girl; and to the youngest, which was the maiden, no beatings and three meals, for he could not bring himself to have the maiden beaten.

Tale #112; **The Cabbage-Donkey**

Intent: To punish someone who has wronged you, particularly if they used magic against you.
Ideal Timing: This spell can be cast any time.

Materials:

Black yarn	A potato	Thumbtacks or thorns

Acquire a potato. Any variety or size will do. This will be your poppet. If you want the spell to work quickly, a small variety like fingerlings might be advisable. Use a larger one if the spell needs to have more punch. The larger the transgression, the larger the potato should be.

Cut five 6" lengths of black yarn. Tie the ends together with three overhand knots so that about 4" of yarn remains free. Tie three evenly-spaced knots along the length of each of the individual strands, with the final knot being close the free end. This is a basic scourge and can be used for several types of baneful magic or heavy cleansing spells.

With a sharp knife, cut the target's name into the potato. If you don't wish to use a knife, you can write the target's name on the potato with a permanent marker. There's not much need for a naming incantation with this type of poppet. The name itself is sufficient.

Every day, take the scourge and beat the potato poppet. For best results, give strokes in multiples of three. When you finish, push a thumbtack into the potato. Continue this until the potato is completely covered in thumbtacks, then discard it with your garbage.

Spell Creation Worksheet

Title of Tale: _____

Inspirational Passage: _____
_____
_____
_____
_____

Nature: _____ **Intent:** _____ **Target:** _____

Duration and Timing: _____

Materials: _____
_____
_____

Casting Method: _____

Instructions: _____
_____
_____
_____
_____
_____
_____
_____
_____

Notes: _____
_____

Spell Creation Worksheet

Title of Tale: _____

Inspirational Passage: _____
_____
_____
_____
_____

Nature: _____ **Intent:** _____ **Target:** _____

Duration and Timing: _____

Materials: _____
_____
_____
_____

Casting Method: _____

Instructions: _____
_____
_____
_____
_____
_____
_____
_____
_____
_____

Notes: _____
_____

Spell Creation Worksheet

Title of Tale: _____

Inspirational Passage: _____

_____

_____

_____

_____

Nature: _____ **Intent:** _____ **Target:** _____

Duration and Timing: _____

Materials: _____

_____

_____

Casting Method: _____

Instructions: _____

_____

_____

_____

_____

_____

_____

_____

_____

_____

Notes: _____

_____

Spell Creation Worksheet

Title of Tale: _____

Inspirational Passage: _____
_____
_____
_____

Nature: _____ **Intent:** _____ **Target:** _____

Duration and Timing: _____

Materials: _____
_____
_____

Casting Method: _____

Instructions: _____
_____
_____
_____
_____
_____
_____
_____
_____

Notes: _____
_____

Healing and Hexbreaking

We often find that healing magics work better when the intended recipient is both aware of and willing to accept the spell or ritual. Active consent and, if possible, participation should be sought by the caster prior to the spell being cast- not for any moral reason, however. This is because there is much evidence that a person who is resistant to or not accepting of help will not seek it out or often benefit from it- especially if it is forced upon them. Magical help is often no different, and in its case this resistance may even cause the spell to fizzle or to do more harm than good.

It is also important to respect the beliefs and desires of others in these types of spellcasting, as well. If you wish to help someone heal who you know would be resistant to accepting magical help, you can offer to say a prayer for them or send a general blessing for their good health or speedy recovery instead of doing a full spell or ritual- though it is very important that this is not used as a smoke screen in order to then go and do the healing spell anyway. It is extremely misleading and disrespectful of the person's belief to do so even if you genuinely have their best interests and health in mind. In instances like this, these acts and prayers should always be done in manners congruent with their own faith and using their own Gods and methods when possible.

There is also the subject of magical cures for various illnesses and physical complaints. If you or your near and dear are injured or happen to fall ill, you would be wise to put mundane medical and psychological treatment to use before spellcraft- and instead utilize the spellcraft in order to achieve better healthcare opportunities, financial opportunities to pay for said care, quicken recovery, or even help them to process the things such as the symptoms or pain more easily; much in the same way that it is not practical to try and pray away your head cold, a spell won't get rid of it either. While it is not entirely outside the realm of physical possibility, it is highly unlikely to happen and mundane methods are likely to work faster and better than magical ones.

What we mean by this is that while magic can be a powerful intercessory when one wants to influence chance or create opportunity; modern medicine is there for a reason. Magic is rarely - if ever - effective when one wants to achieve things which are outside of the realm of physical possibility or logic, science, and reason. Medical professionals are far better equipped and capable of dealing with what physically or mentally ails you- far more so than a healing spell or some Witch on the internet (including us).

When it comes to hexbreaking and the removal of possible enchantments or baneful magics, it is important that- if you have a pre-existing condition that acts up from time to time (i.e. depression, chronic illness, etc), or have recently suffered bereavement or physical injury [sic]- you should go ahead and cite that as the probable cause of any recent curse-aligned misfortune before jumping to hex removal.

Just as it is difficult to determine whether a curse has worked, it is very difficult to determine whether or not a person has been cursed. And while it is tempting to blame misfortune on hexes and such, the truth is that sometimes bad things just happen; this is not to say that curses are not effective, however. It just means that if every unexpected misfortune was the result of ill-wishing, there would be a whole lot of witches doing nothing but muttering jinxes into jars for weeks on end just to keep up.

The Nesting Toad

"And then he said that in another castle the daughter was ill, and they knew no remedy that would cure her." "Oh! the fools!" said the Griffin; "under the cellar-steps a toad has made its nest of her hair, and if she got her hair back, she would be well."

Tale #165; **The Griffin**

Intent: To help cure someone of an illness.
Ideal Timing: Waxing to Full Moon

Materials:

Hair from the target	Clay	Small dish

While some sympathetic magic can be performed with substitutions for material focus, this spell absolutely requires the target's hair to work properly; ball up several strands of the person's hair to form a crude "nest".

Shape the modeling clay into the figure of a squatting toad. It doesn't have to be exact, as long as it is recognizable. Place the clay image of a toad in the "nest" and leave it there for seven days. On the seventh day, remove the clay toad and destroy it. If possible, secretly place the hair under the person's bed to help make them well again.

There is an alternate version of this spell which uses the same materials and methods to inflict illness, rather than cure it. Follow the same steps for healing, but begin during the waning or dark of the moon, and after the seventh day, leave the clay toad in the nest.

To break the curse, follow the steps and timing for the curative version of the spell.

The Water of Life

A King was very ill, and no one believed that he would come out of it with his life. He had three sons who were much distressed about it, and went down into the palace garden and wept. There they met an old man who inquired as to the cause of their grief. They told him that their father was so ill that he would most certainly die, for nothing seemed to cure him. Then the old man said, "I know of one more remedy, and that is the water of life; if he drinks of it he will become well again; but it is hard to find."

Tale #097; The Water of Life

Intent: To help heal oneself or another of a physical malady or illness. (Note: This generally works best if you're working the charm for someone besides yourself, since the source of the illness does not reside in the caster).
Ideal Timing: Waxing Moon, beginning seven days before the moon is full

Materials:

Poppet	Paper	Writing utensil
Small sauce pot	Spoon	Tweezers
Hyssop, Allspice, Thyme, Rosemary, and Ginger Root; 1 oz of Whiskey is optional		

Create or obtain a cloth poppet. For this particular spell, cloth is important because of the method of delivery for the healing medium. The poppet needs to be able to absorb liquid by the spoonful. It does not need a face, but you may wish to mark out a mouth with ink or thread.

Mix together 1 tsp each of dried Hyssop, Rosemary, and Ginger Root. Add to this about half a dozen whole Allspice berries or ½ tsp Ground Allspice. Simmer 1 tbsp of the herb mixture per 1 cup of water for about 15 minutes, then strain to remove the herbs. Set the infusion aside to cool, then bottle it immediately and store it in the refrigerator. It will keep for a little over a week, just long enough for you to work your spell. If you are of legal age to purchase alcohol, you may also add 1 oz of whiskey to the infusion for added punch.

On a small piece of paper, write the name or description of the malady being suffered by the person you seek to heal. Open the poppet's chest and place the paper inside, then close up the slit with loose stitches; you will be retrieving this paper later. Hold the poppet in your hands and name it to represent the target.

Beginning on a waxing-moon night seven days before the moon is full, feed the poppet three small spoonfuls of the Water of Life each evening. During the day, leave the poppet out somewhere that it will be touched by direct sunlight. A windowsill is ideal, but a surface that receives plenty of sunlight works just as well. You may wish to put a towel under the poppet's head to serve as a pillow and to keep any liquid from seeping onto the surface where it lies.

On the night of the full moon, feed the poppet one last dose of the healing infusion, then carefully open the stitches in the torso and extract the paper slip with tweezers. It is important that you do not touch the paper with your bare skin. The paper slip can then be burnt to ash in a fire-safe dish or flushed down the toilet to dispose of the illness, whichever is easiest for you to accomplish; the poppet can be cleansed with salt and used for future healing spells. Any remaining Water of Life should be discarded, as it will not keep.

The Bloody Egg

When he had given her the keys and the egg, and had left her, she first put the egg away with great care, and then she examined the house and at last went into the forbidden room. Alas, what did she behold! Both her sisters lay there in the basin, cruelly murdered, and cut into pieces. She began to gather their limbs together and put them in order, head, body, arms, and legs. And when nothing further was lacking, the limbs began to move and unite themselves together, and both maidens opened their eyes and were once more alive.

Tale #046; **Fitcher's Bird**

Intent: To heal a loved one who has been grievously injured.
Ideal Timing: Waxing or Full Moon

Materials:

Poppet	Paper	Writing utensil
Red food dye	Scissors	Towel
Spoon	Small bowl	Whole egg
Willow Bark, Chamomile, Almond, and Hyssop; plus 1 cup of Vinegar		

Create or obtain a cloth poppet or doll. If you are making the poppet yourself, leave it partially disassembled, with the head, torso, and limbs separate. If you have a pre-made poppet, carefully cut it apart with a pair of scissors.

Combine 2 parts Willow Bark, 1 part Hyssop, and 1 part Chamomile. Remove some of the stuffing from the torso and replace it with pinches of the herb mixture until it is full. Stuff one whole almond into each piece of the poppet. Write the name of the person you seek to heal on a piece of paper and place that in the torso as well.

Assemble the poppet on a flat surface with the various parts in their proper places, but do not sew it up yet. First, name the poppet to represent the target then carefully sew the poppet back together with the herbs and name slip inside.

Add 10-15 drops of red food dye to the cup of vinegar and stir it well. Place the egg in the cup and let it sit for several minutes until the shell turns a deep red color, the darker the better. If you need to add additional food dye, do so. Once the egg is dyed, let it dry thoroughly, then rub it over the reassembled poppet. Pay careful attention to the resewn seams and the part of the poppet where the target person is injured. As you do so, recite seven times:

*By bloodied egg and hyssop's might,
I take from you this painful blight.
By stitching thread and willow's bark,
I give to you the healing spark.*

When you finish, quickly take the egg from your house and discard it. You can either pitch it into a trash receptacle or throw it away toward the west. Either way is effective. The point is that the egg must be out of your house and out of your hand as quickly as possible. Tuck the poppet away somewhere that it won't be disturbed. Once the person is healed, the poppet can be cleansed with salt and used for future healing spells. The herbs and almonds stuffed inside may remain to help with this.

'Neath the Lime Tree's Shade

"Alas!" said she, "I believed him true to me, but he has forgotten me." Next day [her bridegroom] again came along the road. When he was near her she said to the little calf, "Little calf, little calf, kneel by my side, And do not forget thy shepherd-maid, As the Prince forgot his betrothed bride, Who waited for him 'neath the lime tree's shade." When he was aware of the voice, he looked down and reined in his horse. He looked into the girl's face, and then put his hands before his eyes as if he were trying to remember something, but he soon rode onwards and was out of sight. "Alas!" said she, "he no longer knows me" and her grief was ever the greater.

Tae #186; **The True Bride**

Intent: To heal oneself after heartbreak.
Ideal Timing: Waning moon, to draw away the heartache.

Materials:

Knife	A lime	Paper and writing utensil

Acquire a medium-sized lime, a small piece of paper, and a pen or marker. Draw a heart on the paper and write your ex's name inside. You can talk to the paper or cry over it if you need to, whatever will make you feel like you have some closure.

With a small, sharp knife, cut a plug out of the side of the lime. Fold up the paper and tuck it into lime, then replace the plug. Hold the lime in your hands and say goodbye, then take the lime from your home and bury it somewhere off the property or discard it with the trash.

As the lime rots, your heartache will ease.

The Sorrow Pot

Then said he, "If you will not tell me anything, tell your sorrows to the iron-stove there," and he went away. Then she crept into the iron-stove, and began to weep and lament, and emptied her whole heart, and said, "Here am I deserted by the whole world, and yet I am a King's daughter, and a false waiting-maid has by force brought me to such a pass that I have been compelled to put off my royal apparel, and she has taken my place with my bridegroom, and I have to perform menial service as a goose-girl. If my mother did but know that, her heart would break."

Tale #089; **The Goose Girl**

Intent: To relieve your sorrows and bring justice for a grievance.
Ideal Timing: Waning Moon

Materials:

Small sauce pot	Bayberry candle	Fire safe dish
Willow Bark, Rosemary, Majoram, Ground Clove, and Ground Allspice		

Obtain a small pot or saucepan. If neither of these are available, a teapot or a large mug will do. This will be your sorrow pot. It is important to note that after performing this spell, you should wash and thoroughly cleanse the item to make sure that none of your sorrows remain before using it for mundane cooking or other magic. Whisper your sorrows into the pot. Take as long as you like and be as sad or as angry or as vulgar as you feel you need to be. If you shed any tears, try to catch a few of them in the pot for additional potency.

Gather a Palmful of Willow Bark, a Pinch of Dried Rosemary, a Pinch of Dried Marjoram, and a Spoonful of Shavings from a Bayberry Candle, and place them all in a pot. Stir the contents with a spoon until well combined, then tip the whole mixture into a fire-safe dish, carry it to a clear area without fire hazards, and set it alight. The candle shavings will help the herbs to burn more thoroughly, and you can add drippings from a bayberry or black wax candle if you wish to help it along. Carefully sprinkle a generous pinch of Ground Allspice or Ground Cloves into the burning material. Let the herbs burn to ash, then cast the ashes into the wind.

If you stop there, the spell works to relieve sorrow and emotional pain, and to aid recovery and mental clarity. If you wish to go one step further and seek justice for the harm that caused your pain in the first place, add the following incantation as you sprinkle the Allspice or Cloves into the burning herbs. Recite over the flames:

> *The pain I've suffered is your doing*
> *This spell shall be the undoing of you*
> *By sea-salt tear and burning flame*
> *The harm you've done returns to you*

Once the herbs are completely burned, take the ashes and cast them into the wind to carry the spell to its' intended target.

All Heads Off But Mine

The Kings, Princes, and councilors who were assembled there, ridiculed and mocked him, but he did not trouble to answer them, and said, "Will you go away, or not?" On this they tried to seize him and pressed upon him, but he drew his sword and said, "All heads off but mine," and all the heads rolled on the ground. And he alone was master, once more King of the Golden Mountain.

Tale #092; **The King of the Golden Mountain**

Intent: To take back your personal power when it has been stolen from you.
Ideal Timing: Waxing or Full Moon

Materials:

Paper	Writing utensil	Sissors

On a piece of paper, make a list of the people who are stealing your energy or your power. Include people who consistently make you feel angry, frustrated, insignificant, hopeless, despondent, lonely, or worthless. The list can be as long as it needs to be.

When you're finished, read the list aloud, just to cement the names in your mind. Then fold the paper in half and say, loud and firm:

ALL HEADS OFF BUT MINE!

Tear or cut the paper to pieces. The shreds may be retained in a jar to trap the offending parties, or burnt to ash or flushed down the toilet to prevent them from doing further harm.

Seven-Year Bath

At length, as the last day of the seven years dawns, Bearskin went once more out on the heath, and seated himself beneath the circle of trees. It was not long before the wind whistled, and the Devil stood before him and looked angrily at him; then he threw Bearskin his old coat, and asked for his own green one back. "We have not got so far as that yet," answered Bearskin, "thou must first make me clean." Whether the Devil liked it or not, he was forced to fetch water, and wash Bearskin, comb his hair, and cut his nails. After this, he looked like a brave soldier, and was much handsomer than he had ever been before.

Tale #101; **Bearskin**

Intent: To cleanse oneself of magical sludge or negative energy.
Ideal Timing: This spell can be performed anytime.

Materials:

Cloth bag	Pitcher	1 cup of dry oatmeal
Fennel, Hyssop, Lemon Peel, Peppermint, Rosemary, Wintergreen, Salt		

In a bag, combine seven generous pinches of the herbs. Hang this bag inside a large pitcher, fill the pitcher with warm-to-hot water, and let it steep for 15-20 minutes. You're going to want to leave the pitcher in your bathroom, and put a towel down on the floor.

While the herbs are steeping, prepare a bowl of oatmeal. Let the oats soak until they are reasonably mushy, then remove your clothes, get into the tub, and slather yourself with the oatmeal, being careful to avoid getting it into any orifices or in your hair. Give yourself a good rubdown for a few minutes, then rinse the bulk of the oatmeal from your skin. You may wish to put a strainer over the drain to prevent clogs.

Once you're partly rinsed, fetch the pitcher that's been steeping all the while. This is where that towel on the floor is going to come in handy. Remove the sachet and wring it out. Take the pitcher back into the tub with you and use it to carefully rinse away the rest of the oatmeal. Use more water from the faucet if you need to. Rinse the tub immediately after you finish to avoid having to scrub it out later.

Dry yourself off, wrap up in something comfy, and kick back to enjoy the freshly-cleansed feeling!

The Red Flower

Joringel went away, and at last came to a strange village; there he kept sheep for a long time. He often walked round and round the castle, but not too near it. At last he dreamt one night that he found a blood-red flower, in the middle of which was a beautiful large pearl; that he picked the flower and went with it to the castle and that everything he touched with the flower was freed from enchantment; he also dreamt that by means of it he recovered his Jorinde.

Tale #069; **Jorinde and Joringel**

Intent: To remove an enchantment or bewitchment placed upon another.
Ideal Timing: Waning Moon

Materials:

Jar with a lid		Photo of the Target
Red Aster, Red Geranium, Red poppy, Red Rose, and Vetiver		

Collect the petals of a red aster, a red geranium, a red poppy, and a red rose. Dry them in the sun until completely stiff. Combine these with four pinches of vetiver; if you have difficulty finding all the flower petals, rose petals may be substituted. Roses may also take the place of any flower in other spellwork.

Place the petals and pinches of herb in a jar with a photograph of your lover or loved one who you believe is bewitched. Leave the jar in the sun for three days, then place the photo and the dried herbs in a sachet beneath your lover's pillow.

If your lover is some distance away, retain the photograph in a safe place and either burn the dried petals, which will have absorbed the enchantment, or toss them into fast-moving wind or water to dissipate the spell.

Twelve White Flowers

Now there was a little garden belonging to the enchanted house, in which grew twelve lilies; then maiden, thinking to please her brothers, went out to gather the twelve flowers, meaning to give one to each as they sat at meat. But ass she broke off the flowers, in the same moment the brothers were changed into twelve ravens, and flew over the wood far away, and the house with the garden also disappeared. So the poor maiden stood alone in the wild wood, and as she was looking around her she saw and old woman standing by her, who said, "My child, what hast thou done! Why couldst thou not leave the twelve flowers standing? They were thy twelve brothers who are now changed to ravens forever." The maiden said, weeping, "Is there no means of setting them free?" "No," said the old woman, "there is in the whole world no way but one, and that is difficult; thou canst not release them but by being [mute] for seven years; thou must neither speak nor laugh; and wert thou to speak one single word, and it wanted but one hour of the seven years, all would be in vain, and thy brothers would perish because of that one word."

Tale #009; **The Twelve Brothers**

Intent: To break a baneful spell or glamour that has been cast over a group of people.
Ideal Timing: Full or Waning Moon

Materials:

Cardboard tray	Paper	Writing utensil
Metal spoon	Fire safe dish	Charcoal incense disk
Glass jar	Grill (long-nosed) lighter	A location outdoors
Thistle, Sassafras, Fennel, Vervain, Sage, and Cedar Chips- plus 12 white flowers of any kind		

Before beginning your casting, gather twelve white flowers. Any sort will do as long as there are twelve- and yes, they can all be the same kind of flower if need be. Hang the flowers by their stems in a dry place at room temperature, or remove the stems and lay the flowers in a cardboard tray. The flowers will be ready for the casting once they are completely dried out and stiff to the very tips of the petals. This can take anywhere from a couple of days to two full weeks, depending on the size of the flower. If the whole flower is crunchy, the blossom is ready. If parts of it are still soft or pliable, it needs more drying.

Once you begin the actual setup on the day you intend to cast the spell, you must not speak or laugh for at least forty-nine minutes while you make the preparations and perform the casting, or it will not work.

Prepare an open area free of flammable materials. You'll want to do this outside; there's going to be open flame and a lot of smoke. Place a large fire-safe bowl or dish on a heat-resistant surface, such as bricks or pavement, and put a charcoal disc in the bottom. Take the slips of paper and write down the names of the people who have been bespelled, one name per slip.

Prepare the blend of spell-breaking herbs with 2 parts Cedar Chips, 2 parts Green Sage, 1 part Vervain, 1 part Fennel, 1/2 part Sassafras Leaf, and 1/2 part Thistle Leaf. You don't need very much of the mixture- about a cup or so will do. Divide the mixture in halves. Carefully light the charcoal disc and pour one half of the mixture into the bowl and set the other half aside. Stir the mixture with a long skewer or stick until the herbs begin to burn.

Begin adding the flowers one or two at a time, depending on their size, and the name slips. Stir the bowl and add pinches of the herb mixture as needed to keep the fire going. You may need to re-light the bowl occasionally. This is fine, so long as the material keeps burning. Continue until all of the flowers are burning and most of the herb mixture has been used up.

When all twelve flowers are in the bowl and burning well, let the flowers and herbs burn to ash, stirring as needed. Allow the bowl to cool to a touch-safe temperature before handling. Using the spoon, scrape up the ashes of the burnt herbs and flowers, and transfer them to a bottle or jar for safekeeping.

If this process takes the entire forty-nine minutes, then you may speak again as soon as you are through. If not, remain silent for the rest of the time remaining. You may want to use that time to clean up from your casting.

Sprinkle the ashes where the bespelled people will walk. When they walk over the ashes, the spell upon them will be lifted. If you are working this spell at a distance and this is not an option, cast the ashes into the wind or running water to carry the spell to its targets.

Drown the Witch

When they saw the three servants coming in the distance, and the old woman waddling behind, Lena said, "Birdie, we will never forsake each other!" "No, no! never, never!" replied the little foundling. "Then you shall be changed into a pond, and I will be a duck swimming upon it." The old woman drew near, and as soon as she saw the pond she laid herself by it, and, leaning over, intended to drink it all up. But the duck was too quick for her. She seized the head of the old woman with her beak, and drew it under the water, and held it there till the old witch was drowned. Then the two children resumed their proper shape, and went home with the three servants, all of them happy and delighted to think that they had got rid of such a wicked old woman.

Tale #051; Foundling-Bird

Intent: To turn baneful magic back upon the one who cast it.
Ideal Timing: Full Moon or Dark of the Moon

Materials:

Poppet	Shallow bowl of water	Small mirror
Glue		Duck figurine

Carefully glue a small mirror the underside of a duck figurine. The duck can be made of wood, clay, or stone so long as it doesn't matter if it gets wet. It should be large enough to fill the palm of your hand; if need be, you can create a duck from modeling clay, let it dry, and wrap the body with plastic before performing the spell.

Create a small clay poppet and allow it to harden. If you happen to have a material focus from the target, such as hair or fingernails, you should include it, but it is not required. Hold the poppet in your hands and say:

> *Though you think your curse is dread*
> *I'll turn your magic back around*
> *This duck shall sit upon your head*
> *And hold you under till you drown*

Place the poppet facedown in a shallow bowl of water. Put the duck on top of it so that the mirror is on the poppet and the weight of the duck holds it down. Leave the poppet in the water until the clay dissolves or until the effects of the baneful magic are no longer felt.

Fearless in the Fire

"Listen to me," said the maiden, "when the witch comes, she will give thee all kinds of orders; do whatever she asks thee without fear, and then she will not be able to get the better of thee, but if thou are afraid, the fire will lay hold of thee, and consume thee. At last when thou hast done everything, seize her with both hands, and throw her into the midst of the fire." The maiden departed, and the old woman came sneaking up to him. "Oh, I am cold," said she, "but that is a fire that burns; it warms my old bones for me, and does me good! But there is a log lying there which won't burn, bring it out for me. When thou hast done that, thou art free, and mayst go where thou likest; come, go in with a good will." The drummer did not reflect long; he sprang into the midst of the flames, but they did not hurt him, and could not even singe a hair of his head. He carried the log out and laid it down. Hardly, however, had the wood touched the earth than it was transformed, and the beautiful maiden who had helped him stood before him, and by the silken and shining golden garments which she wore, he knew right well that she was the King's daughter. But the old witch laughed venomously, and said, "Thou thinkest thou hast her safe, but thou hast not got her yet!" Just as she was about to fall on the maiden and take her away, the youth seized the old woman with both his hands, raised her up on high, and threw her into the jaws of the fire, which closed over her as if it were delighted that the old witch was to be burnt.

Tale #193; The Drummer

Intent: To break any curse or baneful magic placed upon you.
Ideal Timing: Full Moon, but can be performed anytime.

Materials:

Poppet	Needle	Sewing thread
Paper	Writing utensil	Fire safe burning area
Angelica Root, Crushed Red Pepper, Mustard Seed, Powdered Nutmeg, and Vervain		

Obtain or make a poppet out of paper or cloth. It does not have to be elaborate or detailed, just person-shaped. Carefully stuff the poppet with pinches of the cursebreaking herbs as you go. You can add dried grass or torn-up cotton gauze as filler if you like. Just before closing the poppet up completely, tuck in a piece of paper with the name of the person who has cursed you. If the person is not known, you can just write "You Who Cursed Me".

Prepare a small bonfire or brazier. Be sure to get the proper permissions you need to do this (some places are very strict about open fires) and be sure to practice fire safety at all times. If you cannot build a fire or light up a brazier, a large firesafe bowl can be substituted, as long as it's on a heatproof surface, such as pavement or stone.

Hold the poppet in your hands and say to it:

> *I will not bend, I will not break.*
> *Your power from you I will take.*
> *I will not break, I will not bend.*
> *Your curse's power is at an end.*

Drop the poppet into the fire and let it burn to ash. Add twigs and kindling as needed until the poppet is completely consumed. Wait until the ashes are cool, then cast them into the wind or into running water. If you know the identity of the person who cursed you, you can also dump a pinch of the cold ashes on their property to send the curse back at them.

Spell Creation Worksheet

Title of Tale: _____

Inspirational Passage: _____
_____
_____
_____
_____

Nature: _____ **Intent:** _____ **Target:** _____

Duration and Timing: _____

Materials: _____
_____
_____

Casting Method: _____

Instructions: _____
_____
_____
_____
_____
_____
_____
_____
_____

Notes: _____
_____

Spell Creation Worksheet

Title of Tale: _____

Inspirational Passage: _____
_____
_____
_____

Nature: _____ **Intent:** _____ **Target:** _____

Duration and Timing: _____

Materials: _____
_____
_____

Casting Method: _____

Instructions: _____
_____
_____
_____
_____
_____
_____
_____
_____

Notes: _____
_____

Spell Creation Worksheet

Title of Tale: _____

Inspirational Passage: _____
_____
_____
_____
_____

Nature: _____ **Intent:** _____ **Target:** _____

Duration and Timing: _____

Materials: _____
_____
_____
_____

Casting Method: _____

Instructions: _____
_____
_____
_____
_____
_____
_____
_____
_____
_____
_____

Notes: _____
_____

Spell Creation Worksheet

Title of Tale: _____

Inspirational Passage: _____

_____

_____

_____

Nature: _____ **Intent:** _____ **Target:** _____

Duration and Timing: _____

Materials: _____

_____

_____

_____

Casting Method: _____

Instructions: _____

_____

_____

_____

_____

_____

_____

_____

_____

Notes: _____

_____

The End…

... For Now

Last Notes and Recommended Reading

We hope that you have enjoyed our book! The majority of spells contained herein were authored by Miss Bree herself, with Anna concentrating on chapter forwards and formatting- plus the occasional spell. All other materials from this point forward are handy quick reference tables and correspondence charts (mostly provided by Bree) gathered largely with help from the following books:

Encyclopedia of Magical Herbs; Scott Cunningham, Llewellyn Publications, 1988.

Garden Witch's Herbal; Ellen Dugan, Llewellyn Publications, 2009.

Cottage Witchery: Natural Magick for Hearth and Home; Ellen Dugan, Llewellyn Publications, 2005.

Garden Witchery: Magick from the Ground Up; Ellen Dugan, Llewellyn Publications, 2003.

Grimoire for the Green Witch; Ann Moura, Llewelyn Publications, 2003.

Mrs. B's Guide to Household Witchery; Kris Bradley, Weiser Books, 2012.

Utterly Wicked: Curses, Hexes, & Other Unsavory Notions, Dorothy Morrison, WillowTree Press LLC, 2007.

The Little Book of Curses and Maledictions for Everyday Use; Dawn Downton, Skyhorse Publishing, 2009.

The Complete Guide to Herbal Medicines; Fetrow and Avila, PharmDs, Pocket Books, 2000.

Rodale's Illustrated Encyclopedia of Herbs; Kowalchik and Hylton (Editors), Rodale Press, 1998.

Deriving Spells from the Analysis of Faery Tales

Faery Tales, especially, can be a wonderful source of inspiration when it comes to the realm of magic. Indeed, it is a portion of what inspired this book in the first place! But how do you get from point A to point B, when all you have sitting in front of you is a very large, rather intimidating book of old stories? It can seem like a daunting task, but it is a relatively simple process if one knows how to approach it, and that is what this section is here to help you with.

When it came to finding the right story, our methods differed from one another's. Bree's method was to read the entirety of the book, then annotate the stories which she believed had potential for a spell. During Anna's time creating spells for The Sisters Grimmoire, however, she started with a single concept; if she were doing a love spell she would therefore start her search by looking for stories which included love, marriage, and similarly related subjects. Once found, she would read through the tale and see if there was a passage that leapt out in any particular manner

Whether you start with a concept or devour them all, however, reading through and familiarizing yourself with the tales doesn't hurt. Indeed, familiarizing yourselves with the stories, their archetypes, morals and lessons, and more will give you a leg up when you finally get around to using them as a foundation for your spells, and will make it a little easier to pick the right story for it.

While reading, though, be sure to keep a careful eye out for any passages which jump out at you or grab your attention. When you find these passages, make note of how they made you feel, what they made you think of, and what your initial magical thoughts were concerning them. After you have these passages in mind, you can get on with examining them more deeply in order to see which ones are actually suitable for inspiration.

Settle on a passage or two and you can go about creating your spell.

Start with a concept, goal, or intent inspired by the passage you chose. Will it be a luck spell- or perhaps a money spell would more suitable? This acts as the foundation around which you will built your spell. Once you have the concept you can determine several different factors:

1. **The nature of the spell:** Is it meant to be Beneficial, Baneful, or even Ambiguous? Is it dual purpose, or only singular?
2. **Who the spell will affect, or who will it be cast on:** Will it be yourself, a stranger, a family member, or someone else entirely?
3. **The scope of the spell:** Will it be for a specific effect or a generalized one- such as luck in business transactions, or luck in general?
4. **The Duration of the spell:** Will it be meant for the long term or a shorter term? Is it meant to only be used once, or can it be repeated as needed?

Some of these answers will come more easily than others, but don't give up. Once you have a rough idea established the process gets much easier. The next consideration becomes the spell ingredients, timing, methods, and other factors themselves which constitute the actual spell. Sometimes, though, answering some of these first may help you easier answer the previous set of questions.

For instance, if (like Bree) you tend to consider the Lunar Phases or (like Anna) the Solar, answering these questions will make it much easier to determine which phase of the cycle is the better option under which to perform your spells. There is no penalty for casting your spell during the "wrong" phase of whichever planetary body, however. In fact, if you're creative you can spin the intent of any spell to fit the current phase or alignment of that particular body.

Using Lunar Phases as an example: Say you want to cast a success spell, but the moon happens to be waning and you don't want to wait two weeks for a waxing moon. Instead of fixing your intent to be "bring me success," try restating it as "remove the obstacles to my success". Likewise, say you want to curse the pants off of someone, but you just missed the dark of the moon. Use the waxing moon to gradually increase the strength of the hex you send at your target instead. Both are examples of fitting your magic to the current phases instead of waiting for the correct phase to roll around for you.

Keep in mind, though, that tying your magic to certain Celestial phases can be an enhancement for your magic it is still far from a necessity or requirement. Your spells will work just as well if you choose not to do so, so don't feel pressured into including any external factors such as this if it doesn't suit your paradigm or the way which you perform magic!

Once all of your particulars are set down, moving on to figuring how you want to accomplish the goal of the spell is the next best step.

1. **Method of casting:** Will it be a visualization spell, a Witch Bottle, a Charm, Spell Jar, or something else entirely?
2. **Materials for the Spell:** Will you use herbs, gems, candles, or other materials, or are these unnecessary?
3. **Sonant components:** Do you want to utilize chants, incantations, or other vocal components? Would you prefer to set the tone with music? Or is peace and quiet better for this spell?

Bree tends to go straight to her herb cabinet and start compounding a powder, charm bag, spell jar, or whatever else she feels is needed for the spell. She also tends to employ candles (mostly black or white), and additives like vinegar, pickle juice, lime and lemon juice depending on what the spell is for. Her spell work also often employs the use of some sort of incantation- usually structured in short, rhyming couplets, but one or two have run long, especially in this book.

Anna, on the other hand, prefers to take her ques from the stories themselves; her favorite method for deriving spells from the tales is to analyze what items were mentioned in the tale itself. Take the early preview spell *The Ring and the Glass* which she released, for instance. The spell is very specific about the colors of the items used, and all of these are derived from the story- which you can easily see in the associated passage included with the spell. Specific words and phrases, too, are often employed and she has incorporated some of these into her spells here. Mostly, though, Anna prefers to employ embroidery and other handwork and crafting methods over the use of vocal and sonant components.

Now that we've gone over it more in depth, let's break that down into more coherent, easy to follow steps.

1. Determine the base purpose of your spell
2. Determine the base nature of your spell
3. Determine who the spell will affect
4. Determine the specifics of the spell's effects
5. Determine how long the spell is meant to work
6. Determine the timing of the spell, if applicable
7. Determine the casting method you will employ
8. Determine what materials, if any, will be used to create a physical representation of the spell

9. Determine the vocal and / or sonant components, if any, which will empower the spell

After all of this is in place you are ready to collect the necessary materials and actually cast the spell if you desire.

If it helps you to do so, we recommend keeping a notebook or journal dedicated to the purpose of recording the particulars; this is especially useful for future reference and in determining how well the spell has worked. We have also included worksheets throughout this book in an effort to provide you with places to record your own Faery Tale derived spells. You may find more of these worksheets at the back of this book, as well as an example sheet to help you fill it out should you wish to use them.

These are our combined methods, however. For some of you, these may not be applicable or helpful. Whatever methods you use to analyze Faery Tales and create your spells, we wish you a happy Casting!

Magical Herbal Index by Purpose

* POISONOUS.
Take protective measures, handle with care, and do not ingest.

** UNSAFE FOR THE FEMALE BODIED
Do not use or handle if pregnant, nursing, or if you suffer from "feminine" hormone based health conditions- such as migraines and ovarian cancers [sic].

The plants listed here should be easy to find either at your local supermarket, farmer's market, or herb seller. With the use of an appropriate field guide for identification, you may also check local parks and wooded areas for fallen leaves and twigs.

This list is not exhaustive; we may have missed herbs that should have been marked or otherwise annotated as unsafe. Other herbs may cause allergic reactions to those with certain allergies (for instance, Mugwort** and similar or related plants will cause a similar allergic reaction in those with Ragweed Allergies) and these herbs have not been marked on this index. Please consult a licensed and trained medical practitioner before topically using or orally consuming any herb on this list that you are not familiar with.

Herbs for Cursing

Arguments; to Cause - Blueberry Leaf or Bark, Lemon Verbena, Peony Seed

Bad Luck; to Cause - Blueberry Bark, Chili Pepper, Cumin, Lemon Juice, Walnut, Wormwood*

Bitterness; to cause – Chicory, Lime, Wormwood*

Confusion; to Cause – Ash of Rosemary, Mistletoe*

Cursing; General - Ash of Roses, Cactus Spines, Lemon Juice, Onion, Potato (for poppet), Thorns, Vinegar

Deception; to Cause - Dogbane

Discomfort; to Cause - Chili Pepper, Cinnamon, Nettle

Discord; to Cause – Blueberry, Black Mustard Seed

Inversion - Ash of Roses, Cinquefoil (with soot),

Isolation; to cause – Ivy, Mistletoe*

Pain; to cause – Cactus, Cayenne, Cramp Bark, Guinea Peppers, Mistletoe*, Thorns

Persuasion – Honey, Licorice, Maple Syrup, Sugar, Thyme

Strife; to cause – Blueberry, Cactus, Lemon Grass, Black Mustard Seed, Nettle, Paprika, Peony Seed, Wormwood*

Herbs for Protection

Banishing - Angelica Root, Bay, Betel Nut, Black Pepper, Cactus Spines, Chili Pepper, Cloves, Cumin, Curry, Morning Glory, Oregano, Sea Salt, Thyme, Tobacco, Vinegar

Baneful Magic; Against – Bindweed, Birch, Bloodroot

Binding – Grass, Honey, Ivy, Lobelia*, Vinegar

Cleansing – Ash, Burdock, Cayenne, Citronella, Grapefruit, Hyssop, Lemon, Lemon Grass, Lemon Verna, Lovage, Marjoram, Peppermint, Pine, Salt, Vervain, White Pepper, Willow

Commanding – Bay, Cardamom, Sassafras, Tobacco, Compassion, Tarragon

Deflection – Agrimony, Bloodroot

Expulsion - Angelica Root, Basil, Black Pepper, Cloves, Cumin, Garlic, Leek, Nettle, Turmeric, Vetiver

Intruders; Against - Angelica Root, Asofoetida, Cactus, Hyssop, Oak

Negativity & Discord; Against – Alkanet, Amber, Angelica Root, Asofoetida, Balsam, Basil, Betony, Birch, Black Pepper, Blessed Thistle, Blue Cohosh, Boneset, Borage, Brimstone, Buckthorn, Calendula, Cayenne, Cinquefoil, Clover Leaf, Coffee, Daffodil, Dandelion Leaf, Devil's Bone Root, Dill, Dragon's Blood Resin, Elder, Eucalyptus, Fennel, Gardenia, Garlic, Gorse, Hazel, Lemon, Lily of the Valley, Marjoram, Oak, Papaya, Peach, Pennyroyal**, Pepper, Rose Geranium, Rosemary, Rue* **, Sage, Sandalwood, Spanish Moss, Tangerine, Tansy, Vetiver, White Willow Bark, Witch Hazel, Witches Burr, Yarrow

Magical Harm; Against – Anise, Bay, Bindweed, Buckthorn, Cinquefoil, Elder, Fennel, Figwort, Flax Seed, Garlic, Hyssop, Ivy, Lady Slipper, Marjoram, Mimosa, Mistletoe*, Mullein, Papaya, Peony, Plantain, Rue* **, Sage, Salt, St John's Wort, Vetiver, Wood Betony, Wormwood*, Yew*

Malevolent Spirits, Against - Aconite*, Agrimony, Angelica Root, Anise, Barley, Basil, Bay, Bistort, Bloodroot, Cactus, Cinquefoil, Red Clover, Garlic, Mugwort**, Oak, Rowan, Sage, Salt, St John's Wort, Tansy**, Vetiver, White Willow Bark, Wood Betony, Yew*

Misfortune, Protect Against - Mistletoe*, Rice, Rose Geranium, Sea Salt

Protection; General – Aloe, Anise, Barley, Basil, Bay, Black Pepper, Blackberry, Blueberry, Buckwheat, Burdock, Caraway, Carob, Cayenne, Chia, Chives, Cilantro, Cinnamon, Cloves, Coconut, Coriander, Cumin, Curry, Dill, Fennel, Flax Seed, Garlic, Ginseng, Juniper Berries, Leek, Lettuce, Lime, Mimosa, Mint, Nutmeg, Radish, Witch Hazel

Protection; Children – Caraway, Cloves, Flax Seed

Protection; During Travel – Fig

Thieves; Against – Aspen, Cactus, Caraway, Cedar Berries, Comfrey, Cumin, Juniper, Juniper Berries, Larch, Mustard Seed, Red Peppercorn, Thistle

Turning - Mustard Seed, White Willow Bark

Unwanted Guests; Against - Chili Pepper, Curry, Devil's Claw, Ivy, Oregano, Rosemary, Thistle,

Unwanted Love; Against - Black Snakeroot, Blue Cohosh* **, Camphor, Carrot, Lemon, Mistletoe*, Vervain

Warding; General - Basil, Black Pepper, Sage, Salt

Herbs for Healing

Accidents; Protect Against – Aloe, Black Cohosh* **

Assault; Protect Against - Heather Blossom, Mistletoe*, Quince

Bereavement; Emotional Healing – Cloves, Sage, Thyme, Willow, Witch Hazel

Calming – Catnip, Chamomile, Lavender, Lemon Verbena

Harm; Protect Against – Amaranth, Amber, Angelica Root, Lucky Hand Root, Quince

Healing; General – Cedar, Cinnamon, Cotton, Cucumber, Ivy, Mint, Olive Oil, Raspberry, Raspberry Leaf**, Rosemary, Sage, Yarrow

Healing; Emotional – Cloves, Lavender, Marjoram, Plum, Rose, Saffron, Tarragon, Witch Hazel

Healing; Physical – Allspice, Almond, Aloe, Apple, Barley, Blackberry, Chamomile, Fennel, Garlic, Ginseng, Hops, Horehound, Hyssop, Lavender, Lemon Balm, Peppermint, Persimmon, Potato, Rose, Rose Hips, Spearmint, Thistle, Willow Bark, Wintergreen

Healing; Recovery – Apple, Fennel, Ginseng, Parsley**, Sage

Health; Restore or Maintain – Caraway, Carob, Chia, Ginger, Ginseng, Pumpkin Seed, Rosemary, Thyme

Hexbreaking - Angelica Root, Chamomile, Chili Pepper, Dill, Elder, Fennel, Garlic, Ginger, Mimosa, Mustard Seed, Nettle, Nutmeg, Papaya, Vervain, Vetiver

Illness; Protect Against – Ash, Coriander, Feverfew, Henna, Juniper, Juniper Berries, Mistletoe*, Onion, Peppermint, Rowan, Rue* **, Spikenard, St John's Wort, Tonka Bean, Yerba Santa

Injury; Protect Against - Mustard Seed, Yerba Santa

Longevity – Anise, Maple Syrup, Peach, Sage

Vitality – Oregano, Parsley, Spearmint, Tangerine

Herbs for Relationships

Arguments, to End – Rosemary, Yarrow

Attraction – Almond, Aloe, Basil, Bay, Cardamom, Catnip, Clover Leaf, Dill, Echinacea, Honey, Lemon, Lemon Verbena, Licorice, Lovage, Marigold, Morning Glory, Myrtle, Oak, Orange, Parsley, Patchouli, Pumpkin Seed, Rose, Savoury, Sugar, Thyme, Tomato, Vanilla Bean, Violet, Willow, Yarrow

Beauty – Apple, Avocado, Coconut, Ginseng, Lavender, Lilac, Magnolia Blossom, Orange Blossom, Peach Blossom, Rose, Vanilla

Chastity – Cactus, Coconut, Cucumber, Pineapple, Witch Hazel

Fidelity – Cardamom, Chili Pepper, Clover, Cumin, Licorice, Lime, Magnolia, Olive, Raspberry Leaf**, Rhubarb, Rose, Rye, Thyme

Friendship – Apple, Cloves, Meadowsweet, Myrtle, Rose

Harmony – Basil, Lavender, Meadowsweet, Oak, Orange, Tea Tree, Violet, Yarrow

Jealousy; Protect Against – Pepper, Plantain

Love; General – Apple, Avocado, Barley, Basil, Beet, Brazil Nut, Caper, Caraway, Cardamom, Catnip, Chamomile, Cherry, Chervil, Chestnut, Chili Pepper, Clover Blossom, Cloves, Coriander, Dandelion, Elm, Endive, Fig, Ginger, Ginseng, Hibiscus, Juniper Berries, Lavender, Leek, Lemon, Lemon Balm, Lettuce, Licorice, Lime, Maple Syrup, Marjoram, Mimosa, Papaya, Pea, Peach, Pear, Peppermint, Pimento, Plum, Poppy Seed, Pumpkin Seed, Quince, Raspberry Leaf**, Rose, Rosemary, Rye, Saffron, Spearmint, Strawberry, Sugar, Tomato, Vanilla Bean

Love; Marriage – Bay, Coriander, Ivy, Lily, Olive, Orange, Rose, Violet, Yarrow

Love; Sexuality – Apple, Asparagus, Parsnip, Pumpkin, Savoury, Sugar, Tomato, Turmeric

Love; Attract – Aloe, Apple, Apricot, Bay, Rose, Savoury, Willow, Yarrow

Love; Forget – Pistachio, Shallot, Vervain, Witch Hazel,

Love; Preserve – Honey, Raspberry Leaf**, Savoury, Sugar

Lust; to Increase – Almond, Apple, Cherry, Ginger, Ginseng, Hibiscus, Honey, Lovage, Pomegranate, Sugar, Vanilla Bean

Peace – Aloe, Apple, Cilantro, Coriander, Hops, Lavender, Lemon Balm, Lemon Grass, Marjoram, Olive, Parsley**, Plum, Rose, Tobacco

Relationships; to End - Lemon Verbena, Lemon Juice, Lime

Sex Magic – Asparagus, Avocado, Parsnip, Pumpkin, Savoury, Sugar, Tomato, Turmeric, Watercress

Herbs for Opportunity

Abundance – Barley, Peppermint, Pine, Poppy Seed, Pumpkin Seed, Rosemary, Sesame, Tea Leaf

Blessing; all-Purpose - Basil, Black Walnut Hull

Blessing; Business – Basil, Bay, Orange, Patchouli, Pine, Plantain, Sarsaparilla, Vetiver, Willow

Blessing; Home - Angelica Root, Apple, Bay, Orange, Parsley**, Pine, Plantain, Sarsaparilla, Vervain, Willow

Change – Anise, Fennel, Ginger, Parsley**, Peppermint, Persimmon, Pine

Courage – Borage, Mustard Seed, Nettle, Pepper, Tea Leaf, Thyme, Tobacco, Turmeric

Creativity – Allspice, Beech, Horehound, Jasmine, Violet, Witch Hazel

Employment – Basil, Meadowsweet, Pecan, Thyme

Job Loss; Protect Against - Pecan

Legal Matters; Justice or Favorable Verdict – Hickory, Lovage, Marigold, Tobacco

Luck; to Increase – Acorn, Alfalfa, Allspice, Aloe, Ash Twigs, Bergamot, Catnip, Chamomile, Cinnamon, Clover, Corn, Cotton, Dill, Fenugreek, Ginger, Lemon, Mustard Seed, Nutmeg, Orange, Parsley**, Persimmon, Pineapple, Poppy Seed, Potato, Quince, Rose Hips, Sesame, Shallot, Star Anise, Strawberry, Thyme, Vanilla Bean, Violet, Wintergreen

Money; to Draw – Alfalfa, Allspice, Almond, Basil, Blackberry, Buckwheat, Cabbage, Cashew, Chamomile, Cloves, Dill, Echinacea, Fenugreek, Flax Seed, Ginger, Grape, Juniper Berries, Lemon, Maple Syrup, Marjoram, Mint, Nutmeg, Olive, Orange, Parsley**, Pea, Pineapple, Potato, Rice, Sesame, Tea Leaf, Thyme, Wheat

Opportunity; to Attract – Basil, Pumpkin Seed, Strawberry

Prosperity – Almond, Banana, Basil, Bay, Brewer's Yeast, Cabbage, Chamomile, Cinnamon, Cloves, Ginger, Nutmeg, Sage

Stability – Pecan, Salt

Strength – Basil, Bay, Borage, Cinnamon, Echinacea, Fennel, Garlic, Mustard Seed, Onion, Oregano, Saffron, Spearmint, Tangerine, Tea Leaf, Thyme, Tobacco, Walnut

Success – Aloe, Apple, Basil, Bay, Cinnamon, Cloves, Fenugreek, Ginger, Lemon Balm, Lovage, Pecan, Strawberry, Vanilla Bean, Walnut

Wishes - Apple Seeds, Basil Leaf, Bay Leaf, Beech, Bergamot, Chicory, Cinnamon, Clover, Cloves, Dandelion Seeds, Dogwood Flowers, Ginger Root, Honeysuckle, Nutmeg, Pecan, Peppermint, Pomegranate Seeds, Sage Leaf, Sandalwood, Spearmint, Straw, Sunflower

Herbs for Divination and Truth Seeking

Clarity - Queen Anne's Lace, Rosemary, Sage

Clairvoyance – Anise, Bay, Lilac, Patchouli, Saffron

Concentration - Mace, Rosemary, Vanilla Bean

Confusion; to Dispel – Basil, Bay, Rosemary, Sage, Tea Tree

Divination – Buckeye, Cherry, Corn, Dandelion, Fig, Flax Seed, Hibiscus, Jasmine, Lettuce, Lovage, Marigold, Mimosa, Mugwort**, Orange, Pomegranate, Tea Leaf, Violet, Willow

Deception; Against – Blueberry, Dogbane

Dream Magic – Anise, Bay, Caraway, Catnip, Elder, Flax Seed, Hibiscus, Hops, Lovage, Marigold, Marjoram, Mimosa, Mugwort**, Peppermint, Rosemary, Sage, Violet

Honesty; to Force - Foxglove*, Galangal

Honesty; General – Borage, Violet

Influence; Against – Amber, Barberry, Sassafras, Sulfur Powder

Lies; to End - Lobelia*, Strawberry

Power Boosting – Cinnamon, Echinacea, Ginger, Lemon Grass, Oregano, Paprika, Rosemary, Star Anise

Psychic Powers; to Enhance – Anise; Cinnamon, Clove; Mugwort**; Wormwood*

Treachery; Protect Against – Blueberry, Foxglove

Truth; to Reveal – Borage, Cherry

Wisdom – Almond, Peach, Sage, Sunflower

Miss Bree's Lunar Chart

Full Moon	Wish-making, blessing, cleansing, manifestation, hexbreaking
Waning Moon	Decrease, loss, repulsion, distance
Dark Moon*	Banishment, baneful magic, deception, finality, resolution
New Moon**	Beginnings, initiation, renewal
Waxing Moon	Increase, growth, gain, attraction
Blue Moon	Extra power boost for all full-moon workings

** **New Moon:** The first sliver of moon visible in the sky after the Dark Moon
* **Dark moon:** No moon visible in the sky

Miss Anna's Solar Chart

Sunrise	Fresh beginnings, rebirth, second chances, revelation
Early Morning	Growth, coming into your own, building, creation
Solar Noon	Extra power boost for all solar workings
Noon	Energy, motivation, empowerment, increase
Late Noon	Decrease, loss of potential, residing, leaving
Twilight	Mystery, obscuring, death, beauty, something new from old things

Miss Anna's Lunar Chart

New Moon	Hiding, secrecy, shadows, privacy, isolation
Crescent	Introduction, opening, creation, beginnings
First Quarter	Recurrence, advancement, progress, increase
Gibbous	Thriving, inheritance, wealth, abundance
Full Moon	Exposure, guiding, direction, illumination, truth, exposure
Disseminating	Trickery, elimination, salvage, loss
Last Quarter	Journey, vacation, travel, disappearance, abandonment, withdrawing
Balsamic	Ending, closure, completion, death, finality

Example Worksheet

Title of Tale: This is where the title of you tale is entered to help you keep track of the stories you are using.

Inspirational Passage: If you found a particular passage to be inspirational, feel free to enter that here. It helps as a quick reference in the future, as well as lending the necessary context to your spell. For the rest of this worksheet we will be using hypothetical information in order to show examples of what information to put where.

_____

Nature: Beneficial   **Intent:** Healing   **Target:** Another

Duration and Timing: How long will it take, and when is best? Example: 3 days; repeated each day at solar noon

Materials: What materials will you use? Are there any materials or colors mentioned in the story? How could you use those in your spell? Example: Lavender, a white candle, gold thread.

_____

Casting Method: Is it a visualization, Herb Bundle Charm, Candle Spell, etc?

Instructions: Place your instructions for the preparation of the materials and the casting of the spell in this area here. Make it as detailed or simple as you would like.it to be. If you're writing for yourself only, feel free to use simplified instructions or shorthand to record your instructions.

_____
_____
_____
_____
_____
_____

Notes: Include any reminders or additional notes here if you feel you need them.

_____

Spell Creation Worksheet

Title of Tale: _____

Inspirational Passage: _____
_____
_____
_____

Nature: _____ **Intent:** _____ **Target:** _____

Duration and Timing: _____

Materials: _____
_____
_____

Casting Method: _____

Instructions: _____
_____
_____
_____
_____
_____
_____
_____
_____

Notes: _____
_____

Spell Creation Worksheet

Title of Tale: _____

Inspirational Passage: _____
_____
_____
_____

Nature: _____ **Intent:** _____ **Target:** _____

Duration and Timing: _____

Materials: _____
_____
_____

Casting Method: _____

Instructions: _____
_____
_____
_____
_____
_____
_____
_____
_____

Notes: _____
_____

Spell Creation Worksheet

Title of Tale: _____

Inspirational Passage: _____
_____
_____
_____

Nature: _____ **Intent:** _____ **Target:** _____

Duration and Timing: _____

Materials: _____
_____
_____

Casting Method: _____

Instructions: _____
_____
_____
_____
_____
_____
_____
_____

Notes: _____

Spell Creation Worksheet

Title of Tale: _____

Inspirational Passage: _____
_____
_____
_____
_____

Nature: _____ **Intent:** _____ **Target:** _____

Duration and Timing: _____

Materials: _____
_____
_____

Casting Method: _____

Instructions: _____
_____
_____
_____
_____
_____
_____
_____
_____

Notes: _____

Made in the USA
Lexington, KY
17 April 2016